Y.O.U.

(Your Own Universe)

DISCARDED

Cover Artist
Wouldn't it be great to start your career at fifteen?
That's what illustrator Leslie Cober did when she
sold her first drawing to the *New York Times*.
She's been having fun as an artist ever since.

ISBN 0-673-80044-X

Acknowledgments appear on page 128.

345678910RRS99989796959493

Y.O.U.

(Your Own Universe)

▟ ScottForesman

A Division of HarperCollins*Publishers*

Contents

Fitting In

from *The Kid in the Red Jacket* by Barbara Park

I waited until the movers left before I went up
to my room. I guess I should have told them
where I wanted my bed and stuff, but I didn't.
What difference did it make? No matter where
they put my furniture, it still wouldn't feel like
my room.

To me what's really important is how a room
feels, not where the bed is. Parents don't always
understand stuff like this. To them the most
important thing about a room is how it looks.
Whether or not you've picked up your underwear,
stuff like that. But I wouldn't care if my
underwear was stacked to the ceiling as long as
my room felt right. I want a room where I can
go and shut the door and feel like I've just

closed out the whole world, where I can cry into
my pillow or make faces at my mother.

The trouble was that my new room was so
big, when I closed the door it seemed like half
the world was still in there with me. My mother
could be lurking around and I could be making
faces and not even see her! My closet alone was
practically the size of my old bedroom. I know
big closets are supposed to be real great, but
personally I like my closets small. When your
closet's too big, dead guys with hatchets can
hide in them. It doesn't matter that you know
dead guys with hatchets aren't real. When
you're awake at midnight, even a pretend dead
guy can be scary business.

Sometimes I have an overactive imagination.
It's hard to admit this, but even the bathtub in
my new house scared me. It was the old-fashioned
kind. Instead of looking like a normal bathtub,
it had four legs with claws on the bottom.
The first time I took a bath, I was practically
positive the tub took a step backward.

I didn't bother telling anyone. Why should I?
When you have an overactive imagination, no
one believes anything you say, even if it's true.

The tree outside my window

If King Kong reached in my window and squished me to death, my father would think I squished myself.

That night I hardly slept at all. I was scared to death. The more I thought about my closet, the more nervous I got. Not only could *one* dead guy live in a closet that big, a whole *bunch* of them could probably squeeze in there together. Take vampires, for instance—my closet could hold three to four coffins easily.

Also, it didn't help matters any that my windows didn't have curtains on them yet. I could look outside and see the tree perfectly. It didn't look like a tree, though. At night it looked like a huge ghost with twisted arms and bony knuckles. I figured it was probably waiting for me to go to sleep so it could reach inside and tickle me.

The other thing that drove me crazy was wondering where George Washington slept. My father might have been kidding, but it didn't make any difference. Even if old George never slept in my room, who knows how many other dead people did? I know they weren't dead when they were sleeping here, but they're dead now. What if they left something in the closet and came back to get it? What would I do if some dead colonist came back for his pillow or something?

When my mother got me up the next morning, I was still a little jumpy. My body felt tired, but my eyes were darting around all over the place.

"Well, you look alert this morning," said Mom cheerfully. "All ready for your big day?"

Big day? I thought. *What big day? Wasn't yesterday my big day?*

My mother started looking through the boxes of clothes still heaped in the middle of my floor.

"What do you want to wear today, Howard? Jeans okay?"

I grunted. What did I care what I wore? I didn't know anyone in Massachusetts. It's not like I was expecting a lot of visitors. As a matter of fact, I wouldn't have minded spending the day in my Porky Pig pajamas.

"Well, what's it going to be?" persisted Mom. "What do you think the other kids will be wearing?"

That's when everything clicked. She was sending me to school! It was the first day after the move, and she was actually sending me to school!

I should have known she'd pull a trick like that. I've got the kind of parents who think that if you miss a day of school, you automatically turn dumb. I can't even fake being sick. I have to prove it. I either have to have a fever or junk on my tonsils. If my nose fell off in the middle of the night and I didn't have a fever, I'd have to go to school and breathe through my mouth.

Anyway, after I found out I was going to school, I started feeling really sick. It wasn't like I was actually going to throw up or anything. This kind of sick made my mouth dry out, my stomach churn, and my skin sweat. Just the kind of stuff a new kid needs to make a good impression. . . .

I couldn't eat my oatmeal at breakfast. I've always thought oatmeal looks a little like slop, and my poor stomach just couldn't handle it.

As we drove to school my father kept whistling cheerfully, like we were the Seven Dwarfs going off to work. He went up to the classroom with me, but he wasn't much help. He said, "Hello, I'm Cliff Jeeter and this is Howard." Then he left. Thanks for the support, Dad.

My teacher's name was Mrs. Walton. She smiled at me and welcomed me to the school. I tried to smile back, but my mouth was so dry, my top lip got stuck on my gums. I must have looked like I was making faces at her.

She seemed nice, but I knew that didn't mean much. Teachers are always nice when you first meet them. Their true personalities don't come out until something goes wrong in the classroom, like when a fight breaks out during a spelling bee.

Everyone staring

Anyway, Mrs. Walton talked to me for a few minutes. Mostly she just said a bunch of stuff about how "delighted" she was to have me in her class.

"Heh, heh." I laughed nervously. I sounded like a real lunkhead.

Finally, she assigned me to a desk. It was just in time too. As I sat down the other kids started coming into the room.

I've thought about it a lot since then, and I've decided that the hardest thing about being a new kid is that everyone gawks at you. The way the class was staring at me, you might have thought they'd never seen dry gums before.

Why did it have to be that way? Would it have been such a big deal for them to have just said hi? I'm not asking for a welcoming speech—just "hi," that's all, and maybe somebody to show me to the bathroom.

Of course, by the time lunch hour came, no one seemed to notice me at all. It was like I suddenly disappeared. As we were walking to the cafeteria, two kids actually turned their heads away when I looked at them. I guess they thought I was going to try to eat with them or something.

When we got there, I was forced to ask a little kid from another class what to do.

"Hey," I said, tapping him on the shoulder. "Where do you get milk?"

"From a cow, stupid!" he yelled.

I glared at him for a second. I don't usually carry a grudge, but in his case I decided to make an exception. I'm going to wait until I get to be about two hundred pounds. Then I'm going to come back and stomp him into the playground.

Lunch was awful. I ended up sitting at a table all by myself with no milk. My mother had packed a sandwich and stuff, but I was too upset to enjoy it. Mostly it just tasted like lump.

The thing is, when you're eating by yourself, you keep thinking everyone's talking about why you don't have any friends. You look like a real loser, and you feel lonely as anything. It's funny. I used to think that lonely was something you felt when you couldn't find anyone to play with. It's not, though. Even in a lunchroom crowded with kids, you can feel lonely. Loneliness can strike anywhere—just like the stomach flu.

After I finished swallowing my lump, I wasn't sure what to do with my trash, so I just left it on the table. On my way out the cafeteria door, some man grabbed me by the back of my collar. He didn't say anything. He just spun me around and pointed at my trash.

I would have appreciated it if he'd have told me what I was supposed to do, but he just kept pointing. Finally I walked over and picked it up.

"I'm new," I explained nervously.

Without saying a word, he pointed to a big orange can with a smiley face painted on it.

"Oh," I said, meekly dropping my garbage inside. I had seen the can, but I wasn't sure if it was for trash. "Where I come from, garbage cans don't look that happy," I explained.

Recess was practically worse than lunch. I just sort of wandered around, trying to look like I fit in somewhere. I made a lot of trips to the water fountain. When you go to the water fountain a lot, it looks like you're playing hard and getting thirsty. You've got to be careful, though. After a few minutes your stomach starts to slosh.

I noticed that a bunch of guys from my class had grabbed a ball and were playing soccer across the field. It really made me homesick for Arizona. All I could think about was Roger and Thornsberry and the fun we'd had together on the soccer team. I wondered what the two of them were doing and if I would ever see them again. I wondered if they missed me as much as I missed them. As a matter of fact, I wondered about them so much that, after a while, I wondered if I was going to start to cry.

"Hi!"

The voice behind me sounded familiar, but I knew it wasn't meant for me. How could it be? I was a new kid. No one talks to new kids.

"Hi, I said!"

No one except Molly Vera Thompson, that is. Suddenly the voice was unmistakable.

I turned and looked down. "Oh, it's you," I muttered glumly.

It wasn't a very friendly greeting, but that's the kind of thing you say when you're depressed.

Molly wrinkled her nose cutely and smiled. She was holding hands with someone.

"This is my friend Sally!" she informed me cheerfully.

Sally look scared. Like she thought I might hit her.

"What's wrong with her?" I grumbled.

Molly just giggled. "She's afraid of big kids. One stole her sandwich this morning. I told her *you* wouldn't, though. You're my new friend, Howard Jeeper."

"Jeeter," I corrected, beginning to feel annoyed.

"Jeeper!" Molly repeated cheerfully. "I like Jeeper better."

"It doesn't matter what you like better. You can't go around calling people the wrong name."

"Why?"

"Because it's wrong," I snapped.

"I know that," she retorted. "But I like Jeeper better anyway."

By now I was almost yelling. "Fine! Call me any stupid thing you want! But it's wrong!"

"I know that! You already told me that!"

Suddenly Sally started to cry. Then she sort of huddled over like she was going to get punched out.

"Trouble here?" bellowed a deep voice behind me.

Slowly I turned and looked up. It was the same teacher who had grabbed me in the cafeteria. Geez! What was wrong with this guy, anyway? Who did he think he was . . . Rambo?

Quickly Molly grabbed my hand. "Nope. No trouble. I'm Molly Vera Thompson and this is my new friend, Howard Jeeper. Only I'm not supposed to call him that, only I like it better."

The man frowned and looked at Sally. "What's she crying for?"

Then the three of us just stood there for a second, watching Sally bawl. Molly shrugged. "Maybe she's crying because she had to eat hot lunch today."

Finally the man just sort of pointed his finger in my face and walked away. If you ask me, some teachers take playground duty too seriously.

As soon as he was gone, I pulled my hand away and put it in my pocket. "Look. Why don't you two just go swing, or something?"

Molly shook her head. "Nope. Can't," she announced. "I don't get to swing for a week. On Friday I pushed Frankie Boatwright off the swing, and now Teacher said I have to learn a lesson."

"Fine. Go seesaw, then," I retorted.

"Nope. Can't do that, either. I'm not sure what I did wrong there. All I know is, Teacher

Guys playing soccer.

Molly
and Sally.

Yuck!

said I can't teeter-totter again until I can act like a lady."

By now I was feeling pretty frustrated. This was exactly what I needed—two little first-grade girls following me all over the playground.

"Look, I gotta go, okay? You two run along and do whatever it is you do."

Suddenly Molly's face grew serious. "You can't go anywhere, Howard. When you're at school you have to stay at school. If you try to go home, the principal will track you down with radar. Frankie Boatwright told me that."

Finally I just took off running. If I didn't, I was going to go crazy. I didn't even think about where I was headed; I just ran around the playground for a minute and then onto the soccer field.

Before I knew it, someone was passing the ball to me. I guess all my frustration had built up inside, because when I kicked the ball, I booted it so hard that it sailed right over the top of the net. It was probably the hardest I've ever kicked in my whole life. The bell rang then. But on my way back to class two kids came up to me and said, "Nice kick."

Maybe it doesn't seem like much, but those two words were the best things I'd heard in a long time.

Thinking About It

1. Howard sounded like a real lunkhead when he laughed in front of the teacher. He said so himself. Most likely, *you've* never felt this way. But just in case, if what happened to Howard happens to you, give yourself some advice.

2. "Hi!" With that one word, the mood of the story changes. Find other places where one word or one little incident changes the mood of the story.

3. You are a student in Howard's class. How can you make him feel welcome?

Another Book by Barbara Park

A boy's sense of humor helps out in sports, and dealing with a bully, in *Skinnybones*.

Two Friends

by Nikki Giovanni

lydia and shirley have
two pierced ears and
two bare ones
five pigtails
two pairs of sneakers
two berets
two smiles
one necklace
one bracelet
lots of stripes and
one good friendship

Winter Poem

by Nikki Giovanni

once a snowflake fell
on my brow and i loved
it so much and i kissed
it and it was happy and called its cousins
and brothers and a web
of snow engulfed me then
i reached to love them all
and i squeezed them and they became
a spring rain and i stood perfectly
still and was a flower

No Talking!

by Nikki Giovanni

It was 1952. We were all afraid. We knew that the fourth grade would be different from the earlier grades. In fourth grade we'd read hard books and write reports. We'd be loaded down with homework too.

Then there was Miss Piersall. For one thing, she kept a long ruler on her desk; for another it was said she didn't like recess. I wasn't too worried about the work; the teacher told you what to do and you did it.

My mom taught third grade, so I usually beat her home. By the time she got there, my homework was waiting for her and on my days to do so the dusting and dishes were done; the garbage taken out; Duke, our dog, was fed. It's not that I was a "good" girl so much as I couldn't, and can't stand being fussed at. And worse than the words was that "you've-let-me-down look." I hated that look more than anything.

One day Miss Piersall had a teacher's meeting. (At my school, St. Simon's Episcopal, the nuns liked to meet during the day.) The instructions were No Talking. I didn't talk, but the fourth grade could be heard all over the building. When Miss Piersall came back to class she was very angry. "I'm going to give each one of you a swat," she said. I raised my hand. "Nikki?" "I wasn't talking, Miss Piersall. I shouldn't be swatted," I said. "But you know who was, don't you?" she asked. That didn't seem fair to me. Of course I knew. But I didn't tell. And I was given one swat.

I never forgot what happened in Miss Piersall's fourth grade class that day. I am a writer because I believe fairness should be accorded the individual.

Musical Pals

from *Between Old Friends* by Katherine Leiner

Every single day of my life I practice on my violin. Even on Saturdays and Sundays. It takes a lot of my time. Mostly, I don't mind because I like my violin. But sometimes I get sick of it. Then, I feel like quitting. Last Tuesday was one of those times.

I was waiting for the bus. I saw these kids skateboarding and having fun. I thought how I'd like to be able to go home, have a snack, and play around till dinnertime. Instead, I was waiting for the bus to take me to my violin lesson. Yuck.

That day, when the bus pulled up, I thought about not getting on. But then I did. I showed the driver my pass and started back to my usual seat. As I got close, I saw a man sitting in it. But there was an empty seat next to him. As I sat down I saw he had a violin case too. We smiled at each other.

"What a coincidence, huh?" he said, pointing to his own case. "How long have you been playing?"

"Two years," I answered. "How about you?"

"Oh, let's see." The old man paused and leaned his head back. "Going on about seventy-five years, now. Give or take a few."

"Seventy-five years! Wow! That's almost forever," I exclaimed.

"Nothing's forever, but you're right, it is a long time." The old man smiled and patted his case. "We've done well for each other, this old fiddle and me. We've had some good fun together. Do you have fun with yours?"

"Most of the time," I said with a sigh. "But it's sure hard sometimes." I thought about the hour I had to practice each day.

"I know what you mean. Practicing takes a lot of time. It keeps you away from friends too," he said. "That's hard."

I thought about what Sarah might be doing. She was probably swinging on the tire out in her backyard.

"When I was ten," the old man said, "I was practicing seven to eight hours a day. For that whole year, I didn't even go to school. I had a private tutor who taught me my schoolwork at home." The old man shook his head.

"When did you see your friends?" I asked.

"I didn't. How could I? There was no time," he added. "I hope you have lots of friends."

"I do," I said.

"You know, whenever I had problems practicing, I would always imagine myself in an orchestra: part of that gigantic sound. I wanted to be good enough for that." He adjusted his

Seventy-five years! Wow! that almost forever.

D·27

collar and glanced out the window of the bus. "I wanted to be good enough to play with an orchestra."

"Are you good enough?" I asked him.

He nodded.

I closed my eyes and tried to imagine myself in our school orchestra, with Kenny on the piano and Mrs. Dixon conducting us.

"Where does your orchestra play?" I opened my eyes and looked the old man straight in the face. He didn't have many wrinkles for somebody who had been playing for seventy-five years. He had to be pretty old.

"I don't play in just one orchestra anymore," he said. "Usually I'm part of a different orchestra each day that's making music for either a movie or TV show. We record the music in a studio and then you hear it when you see the movie or television show." I thought about how much I liked the music in *Star Wars*.

"I had my first recital at six and a half years old." He pulled his wallet out and showed me a photograph. "That's me. All dressed up like Buster Brown."

He looked so funny in his short pants and ruffled shirt, I had to put my hand over my mouth to keep from laughing. The styles were sure different back then.

"When I was twenty years old, I took my violin and went to Paris, France, to play jazz. It broke my father's heart. He wanted me to stay home and be a concert violinist. Papa thought playing jazz was a waste of time."

That's me. All dressed up like Buster Brown.

I would always imagine myself in an orchestra: Part of the gigantic sound.

I wasn't sure what jazz was. "Is it a waste of time?" I asked.

"Are you kidding? Jazz is great. And I've played with some of the greatest players ever: Tommy Dorsey and Bunny Berigan and Artie Shaw and there were so many others. It's the kind of music that lets the violin use all of its soul and all of its power." He closed his eyes as if there were jazz playing at that exact minute.

"Who chose the violin for you to play?" he asked me.

I had to think about that one. My mom had wanted me to play the piano. My dad had wanted me to play the clarinet.

"I did," I finally answered.

"Why?" he asked.

"Well," I started. "I guess I like the way it sounds. It kind of makes me happy and sad at the same time."

The old man threw back his head and laughed.

"You know, you're exactly right. I suppose that's the way I've felt all these years," he said. He picked up his case and slowly got to his feet. "This is my stop. If you keep practicing, maybe you'll get to play in an orchestra one day." He turned and walked down the aisle. "I'll be seeing you," he called behind his back.

"Hey, wait!" I called after him. "I don't even know your name."

"Mr. Bluestone," he said and he gave me a quick little bow.

"Nice to meet you, Mr. Bluestone."

I sat down and gave my violin a little pat.

Thinking About It

1. If you met Mr. Bluestone after he performed at your school, what would you ask him about his seventy-five year career as a violinist?

2. Why would someone use their free time to practice a musical instrument for hours and hours a day? How would Mr. Bluestone answer this question?

3. Suppose you were a musician like Mr. Bluestone and the girl in the selection. What kind of music would you play? Would you play in a symphony orchestra or some other kind of group? Why?

China's Precious Pandas

by Claire Miller

High in the steep and misty mountains of China, a giant panda padded along under the tall trees. She moved silently through the mist. But she stopped often to eat something pandas have been munching on for millions of years: bamboo stalks. All she wanted was to eat, and eat some more.

The year was 1980, and not many giant pandas were left in the wild. But this panda didn't know that she and other pandas were in trouble. She led a peaceful life, living by herself most of the year. She wasn't even on the lookout for dangerous animals—she had never met an animal that dared to attack her.

The barrel-shaped panda often sat on her rump while she ate. Then she could use her forepaws like arms to bend the bamboo stalks toward her mouth. Before eating a stalk, she would usually peel off the covering. The stem inside was tough and woody. But her strong jaws and teeth were able to crunch off bite after bite of the tough plants.

As the panda went quietly about her business, she sniffed the air. She smelled something she liked but hardly ever had a chance to eat: meat! Being so big and bulky made it hard for her to chase and catch small animals. So when she had a chance to eat a dead animal, it was a special treat.

Now the panda followed her nose toward the delicious smell. Finally she found just what she was sniffing for. The piece of meat was hanging inside a strange box made of metal bars. Well, nothing was going to stop this panda! Into the box she went, and a door slammed. The panda was caught in a trap!

After a while, some creatures she'd sometimes seen from far away came right up to the trap. Then she felt something sharp prick her in her leg. Suddenly she became very sleepy. When she awoke, she was able to walk right out of the trap. But now she had a collar around her neck. She pawed at it, but the collar just wouldn't come off. So she headed into the forest and forgot about it.

Follow that panda!

What had happened to the panda? The "strange creatures" that came toward her were scientists. They had come to this bamboo forest, called the Wolong Natural Reserve, to find out all they could about wild pandas.

But first the scientists needed a panda to study. They knew that it wouldn't be easy to get close to a giant panda in the wild. That's why they had set the trap. And that's why they had given the panda a shot of sleeping medicine.

A scientist tracks Zhen-Zhen's
activities by listening to radio signals
coming from a transmitter in her collar.

While the panda was asleep,
the scientists had taken her from
the trap so they could weigh and
measure her. She was an average-sized
panda and weighed 190 pounds (85 kg). They
had also taken a sample of her blood to study.

Next the scientists had put a waterproof radio
collar on the panda. The transmitter in her collar
gave off radio signals that traveled many miles.
By listening for these signals on a special
receiver, the scientists would be able to tell
where the panda was. Also, they could tell what
she was doing, because the radio beeped faster
when she moved than when she was at rest.

The scientists decided to name the panda
Zhen-Zhen. Her name meant "precious" in
Chinese, and it would remind people of how
precious, or valuable, *every* panda was.

The bamboo news

As Zhen-Zhen disappeared into the forest, the
scientists made plans to find out how much food
she ate. So they followed her and looked at her
droppings. They discovered that Zhen-Zhen
left droppings up to 100 times a day. A very

large amount of the bamboo she ate passed right through her body without being digested.

Zhen-Zhen had to eat a lot of bamboo in order to get enough nourishment. Some days she crunched down 88 pounds (40 kg), or about 650 bamboo shoots! And she didn't stop eating just because it was night. She had to fill her belly every few hours.

Zhen-Zhen's secrets

Zhen-Zhen showed the scientists how difficult it is for wild pandas to raise their young. The first spring that Zhen-Zhen was wearing a collar, the scientists noticed by her radio signals that she was moving around more than usual. Some of them decided to see what was going on.

They went to a place where they could watch her. Suddenly, from a mountain ridge above Zhen-Zhen, they heard a male panda singing a "love song" to her. Zhen-Zhen listened as he whined, barked, moaned, and bleated.

The next day the scientists saw her mating with the male, so they hoped that she would have a cub to raise by the end of summer. She did!

Zhen-Zhen's cub was born in a den in a hollow tree. While her cub was in the den, she stayed nearby. Sometimes she took the cub with her, carrying it in one paw while she walked on three. Zhen-Zhen took good care of her cub, but for some reason it died during the winter. Zhen-Zhen's next baby also died. The scientists never found out why.

Pandas raise only one cub at a time, and it takes them about a year and a half to do it. The

A scientist rests at the base of a hollow tree where Zhen-Zhen has slept.

babies often die before they are ready to be on their own. The average wild panda mother is able to raise just one healthy cub every three to four years. That's why there are never many young pandas around and why every panda is precious.

While studying Zhen-Zhen, the scientists learned that big trees are very important in a panda's bamboo forest. Mother pandas need hollow trees for dens. And pandas prefer to eat bamboo that's growing under trees.

Zhen-Zhen also taught the helpers at the scientists' camp a lesson. Once when the scientists were gone for a month, Zhen-Zhen came nosing around the camp. The workers at the camp gave her sugar cane, meat, and bread. Soon Zhen-Zhen started coming every day. She would go inside the tents to *demand* food. She threatened to attack when she didn't get the treats.

When the scientists came back, they were upset. They took Zhen-Zhen far away, where she would return to her wild ways and eat only bamboo again. She had reminded everyone that a wild creature must not be treated like a pet.

Zhen-Zhen was one of several pandas to wear a radio collar in Wolong. Because of the radio collars, the scientists tracked down many panda facts and secrets. They learned things they couldn't find out from zoo pandas, such as how much bamboo forest each panda needs to live in. And they were helped by Zhen-Zhen and the other wild pandas who lived among the misty mountains of Wolong.

Thinking
About
It

1. You are invited to help the scientists study the pandas in the mountains of China. What things will you do on the trip?

2. The scientists spent a lot of time studying Zhen-Zhen and other pandas. What did they learn? How can they use the information to help the pandas?

3. What are some things you can do that might help the pandas survive?

Why We Have Dogs in Hopi Villages

A Legend Told by Arizona Indian Children

Collected by Byrd Baylor

There was a boy about our age. He lived in a
Hopi village way up on the mesa. In those days
the people were always arguing and fussing with
each other and this boy used to say he was going
to find some way to stop all that bad feeling.

He thought that if he went away and saw
another village where people got along better he
could come back and tell his people what to do
and they would thank him.

He knew it would be a long journey. But all
he took with him was a water jar and a loaf of
bread that his mother baked for him.

When he went down the path that led away from his village he did not know which way to go. He just walked where he felt like going. Day after day he walked.

After many days had passed the boy came to the edge of a village he had never seen. It seemed like a happy place where people got along. But as he came closer he could see that it was a village of dogs, not people.

He asked the dogs if he could speak to their chief. Even though they had never seen a human

before, they could tell that this boy came in peace so they let him enter their village.

They took him down the ladder into the kiva where councils and ceremonies are held. The dog chief sat with all his dog councilmen in a circle. The boy joined them in the circle. They all smoked the peace pipe together. Everyone took four puffs and passed the pipe around four times, right and left. The boy smoked with them.

Then it was time to speak. The boy said, "I came to get your help so the people of my village

can find out how to stop arguing and fighting all the time. Maybe some of those dogs will go back with me."

But the chief said, "It will be up to my people. I will have no part in this."

They came out of the kiva together but none of the dogs offered to go with the boy. None of them wanted to leave his own village.

When night came the boy went to a little clearing outside the village and he lay awake for a long time trying to think of a way to get the dogs to go with him.

At last a spirit came down to him from the North Star.

"What do you want?" the spirit asked. "I have all the things that you could want."

The boy did not know what to ask for. But he remembered that many of the dogs looked thin and hungry so he said, "Some food would be good."

The spirit got the food and blessed it. When the boy awoke the food was there beside him. Some of the dogs ran up to the pile of food and began to eat it.

As soon as the boy saw that the dogs were eating the blessed food he knew he had asked the spirit for the right thing. He knew he had found a way to make the dogs follow him.

He went down into the kiva again with the dog leaders of that village. Again they all puffed the peace pipe four times each and again the pipe went around four times, right and left.

Then the boy told the chief, "Some of the dogs ate my food. Those are the dogs that will be willing to go with me. They belong to me now because they took my food."

It was true.

The dogs that had eaten the blessed food gathered around the boy wherever he stood. They followed him all the way to his own village up on the mesa.

He gave one dog to each family. The people were so happy to have the dogs that they stopped quarreling.

Hopi villages have been peaceful ever since.

Now dogs have their jobs here. They guard our houses and our people and go to the fields with us and watch over the sheep. And they still remind us not to quarrel. That is their main job.

Group story, Hopi, *Second Mesa Day School:* Floyd Albert, Marvin Beeson, Renee Cleveland, Maude Dennis, Stephanie Hyeoma, Gene James, Jamie Jimmy, Beth Kachinhongva, Christine Kewenvoyouma, Norene Kootswatewa, Kirk Lomawaima, Judith Namingha, Patrick Secakuku, Winifred Secakuku, Gail Tewawina

How Oceans Came to Be

A Legend Told by Arizona Indian Children

Collected by Byrd Baylor

I'itoi, a Great Spirit of the Papago tribe, knew everything before it happened.

He knew that a flood was going to come and cover the earth, so he wove himself a big watertight basket. He sat in it and floated around during the flood.

After the flood was over, he noticed that the earth was still floating in water. It could not settle in one place.

I'itoi knew what to do. He called the spiders to come and weave webs to hold the land steady. He told them to sew earth and sky together. The spiders worked as hard as they could, but in some places the webs were not strong enough to hold back the water.

Those places can still be seen. They are the lakes and oceans.

Dianne Orosco, Papago, *Phoenix Indian School*

Thinking
About
It

1. "Why We Have Dogs in Hopi Villages" and "How Oceans Came to Be" both tell why or how something happened. What other stories can you recall that remind you of these? In what ways are the stories similar?

2. *Why* stories have been told by people all around the world for many, many years. Why do you think people tell these stories?

3. Make up a story explaining why or how something happens. If you have trouble thinking of a subject for your story, look everywhere around you, and you will see something to make a *why* story about.

Who's the New Kid

(or) Mary Had a Little Problem

with the

by Martha Bolton

Hoofs?

Character: Mary (of "Had a Little Lamb" fame)
Setting: On the road to school
Props: School books
Costume: Dress, shoes, and socks

(Mary, books in hand, enters skipping. She turns to look behind her, then stops and shakes her head in frustration. She then speaks to her lamb who is, of course, unseen by the audience.)

Go on! Get! How many times do I have to tell you, you *can't* come to school with me! You're a lamb! And I don't think lambs are considered foreign exchange students!

So, c'mon! Take off my school sweater and put my bookbag back where you found it. It was a nice try, but Mr. Sternly, the school principal, would never let an animal onto the campus.

Okay, sure, there *are* a few sixth graders he
considers animals, but at least they don't eat the
soccer field.

Now, go on. *(coaxing)* Go on. *(She breathes a
sigh of relief, skips a few steps, then stops and
looks to her side.)* No, no, I meant go *that* way.
(She points in the opposite direction.)

Aw, look, even if you *did* make it past Mr.
Sternly, you don't think you could fool my
teacher, Miss Trebble, do you? She'd notice you
sooner or later . . . like when you started going
"baa" in class, or nibbling on our fungus
experiments. After all, she didn't let me get away
with that, why should she let you?

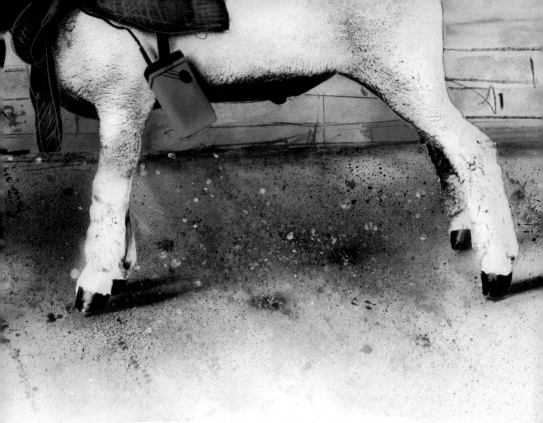

And don't think they're going to serve you grass in the cafeteria. This is Monday. That's Thursday's main course.

So, go now. Get going. *(once again coaxing)* There. That's a good girl. *(to audience)* Hey, it's nothing against her personally. It's just that school's no place for a lamb. I mean, why would a lamb need to learn arithmetic? Unless, of course, she can't get to sleep and has to start counting people. And why should a lamb bother learning cursive writing? Isn't printing good enough? Then, there's peer pressure to consider. Everyone knows sheep just follow the crowd.

No, she's much better off back at home, and she knows it. That's why she finally agreed to. . . . *(looks at her side, then shakes her head)* What are *you* still doing here?! *(to audience)* Oh, well,

what else should I expect from an Obedience School drop-out?

(pleading to lamb) C'mon, you've got to get going before someone sees you with me. There *is* that new leash law, you know. You want me to get fined?

Now, go on. Be a good girl. *(threatening)* Or do I finally get that new wool coat I've been wanting? *(smiles triumphantly)* Aha! I thought that might persuade you. *(Brief pause, then cupping her hands, she yells.)* And don't forget to wait for the crossing guard!

(She gives a deep sigh, then looks out toward the audience.) Whew! That was a close one! *(She starts to continue skipping toward school, then stops suddenly. She turns to the audience.)* Oh, but don't get me wrong. I love her. But I just hope she outgrows this before I go to college! *(She shakes her head, then skips offstage.)*

Blackout

Thinking About It

1. Mary wants to go to school by herself. The lamb wants to go to school with Mary. What would *you* like to happen? Why?

2. It's tough to argue with a lamb. How does Mary convince her lamb to quit following her?

3. Someone else from a nursery rhyme or a fairy tale has a speech to give. Who is it? What do they say?

Early Spring

by Philip Whalen

The dog writes on the window with his nose.

Mouse Under the House

by Arnold Adoff

Mouse   Under The House   Mouse   In The House

One Day   In This Coldest Winter   But In Our
    W a r m
    Kitchen

Daddy   Screamed   A Perfect
Cartoon Scream   And Dropped   The Heavy Cream
And Dropped   His C a k e Pan
    A n d Ran
    Out Of Our
    W a r m
    Kitchen
    Faster Than The Mouse Was
    R u n n i n g The Other Way

Later On   We Explored Outside   And Found A Crack In The
Foundation Stones Big Enough For A Whole Family Of Cold
And Hungry Mice   And All Their Luggage   They Must Have
Traveled Through The Heating Ducts That Lie   Under The
House From Room To Room Until They Settled In The Warm
Kitchen In Back Of The Cabinet Next To The W a r m Oven
Their
Nest Was Between Two Bags Of Daddy's   Best Cake Flour
And An Old Pot Full Of Soft White String I Think
They Were Planning To Stay Until Spring

Turtle

by George Ancona

Watch

Brazil

Praia do Forte

Twice every night during the sea turtles' nesting season, a jeep bounces along the beach of Praia do Forte, and a searchlight sweeps the sands between the jeep and the ocean.

Now Neca and Julio are covering the fourteen kilometers of beach. Later Guy and Alexandre will take the second watch.

The oceanographers are looking for the tracks of a sea turtle. The tracks will lead them to a nest, where they may be in time to find a female turtle laying her eggs.

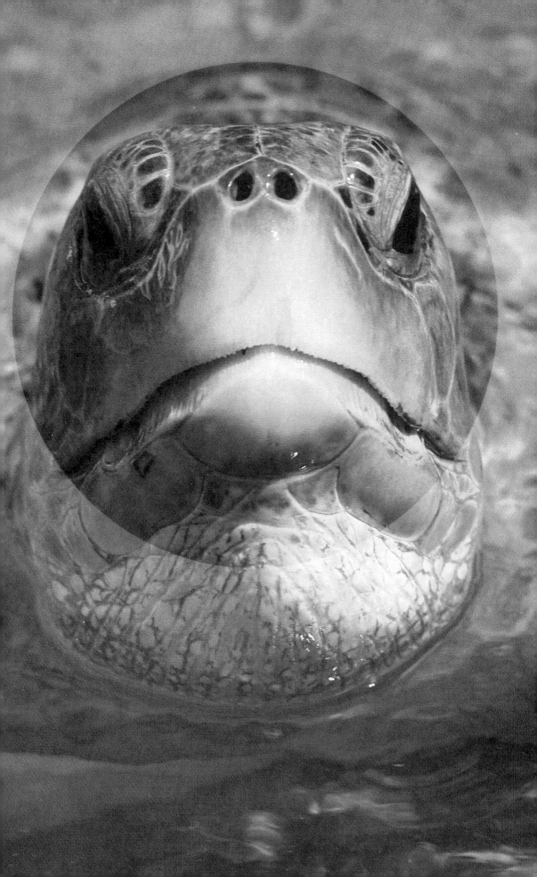

Suddenly, above the roar of the wind and the motor, Julio shouts, *"Tartaruga!"* Neca slams on the brakes and switches off the motor. Dousing the lights, they both jump out into the darkness and scramble silently down the slope to the dark shape on the beach.

While still at a distance, Julio and Neca hear the turtle's flippers scrape the sand. Moving slowly behind the turtle, they turn on a flashlight briefly to see the creature. It is a *Caretta caretta,* or loggerhead turtle. Her shell is encrusted with barnacles. She is building her nest.

The turtle has just finished digging her bed, or body pit, a slight depression in the sand in which she now rests her bulk. She is building her nest above the high-water mark, since saltwater would kill the eggs.

Neca and Julio watch as the turtle begins to dig out the egg cavity. Using her rear flippers, she scoops out a hole in the moist sand. In dry sand, the cavity would collapse.

The turtle raises the front of her body as she works, enabling her to dig a deeper hole. She lifts each flipper full of sand vertically so that she

will not disturb the wall of the hole. By now the cavity is about sixteen inches deep. Finally, the turtle widens the bottom of the hole.

Julio scrapes away some sand beneath the loggerhead to reveal the egg chamber. The cavity completed, the turtle releases a thick liquid from the cloaca, an opening located slightly in front of her tail. This mucous will protect the eggs as they fall and fill the nest.

Now the turtle's body begins to contract, and the first egg drops into the cavity. As the contractions continue, eggs begin to fall at a faster rate. In about twenty minutes, the turtle has laid from one hundred to one hundred and fifty eggs. The eggs are about the size of a Ping-Pong ball, not hard but leathery and flexible.

While the turtle is laying her eggs, she seems to be in a trance. She is not disturbed by the camera or by the flashlight that Julio uses from time to time.

Julio moves in to attach a metal tag to the turtle's right front flipper and to measure her shell. The tag carries a number and a request that anyone finding the turtle advise TAMAR of the tag number, the location of the sighting, and the dimension of the shell. From now on, whenever this turtle is seen nesting, scientists will be informed and will learn more about the habits of sea turtles.

While nesting, the turtle has been secreting a liquid from her eyes. Since turtles live in saltwater, they must eliminate salt from their bodies all the time. What they cannot excrete by urine they eliminate through ducts next to their tear ducts. This process also keeps sand out of their eyes while they are nesting. And it has given rise to the popular story that they are crying from the effort of laying eggs.

Using her rear flippers, the loggerhead now begins to bury the eggs. She gathers sand from the side of the bed and sweeps it into the egg cavity until the hole has been filled. Then she moves forward and uses her front flippers to fill in the entire bed. Almost an hour has passed since Neca and Julio first sighted the turtle.

The turtle seems awake now and aware of her surroundings. Breathing heavily, tired from her efforts, she turns around and begins her return to the ocean. The tracks she leaves parallel those she made when she emerged from the sea. When she reaches the water, she hesitates, lifts her head, then plunges into the waves and disappears.

Neca and Julio know that the turtle will be back. They have learned from the tags on other turtles that she will return to this beach to lay eggs as many as three times each nesting season, which lasts from September through March.

Neca and Julio have followed the turtle to the ocean. Now they go back to the nest for the eggs. If they were to leave them, the eggs might be dug up by other people, or by wild dogs or other animals. With a thin stick, Neca and Julio prod

the nest to locate the egg cavity. Once they feel a soft spot, they start to dig with their hands. Soon the eggs are uncovered.

Making sure the eggs remain at the angle at which they found them, Neca and Julio count the eggs and put them inside a Styrofoam cooler. Julio packs them in moist sand to protect them during the trip back home. Then Neca measures the depth of the egg cavity.

Back at the jeep, Julio makes note of the number assigned to the turtle, its species, the size of its shell, the depth of its nest, and the number of eggs found inside.

Then the scientists return to their base and carefully transfer the eggs to a new nest. They bury the eggs at the same depth at which they found them. There the eggs will be protected from the heat while they incubate for about fifty days.

A metal screen, partially buried, is placed around the new nest. This will keep small animals out and later will keep the hatchlings in.

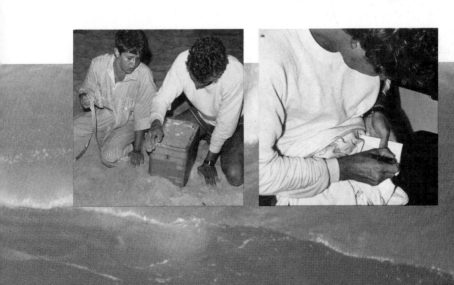

Sea turtle
nesting areas

Brazil

Praia do Forte •

Sea turtles nest along beaches of tropical and subtropical lands. In the Western Hemisphere, these include the beaches of North, Central, and South America and the islands of the Caribbean. The threat to turtles nesting here has been so great that today six of the hemisphere's seven species of sea turtles are considered endangered.

Scientists and conservationists alone cannot save the sea turtles. The people who depend on turtles for their income must help. In the town of Praia do Forte, TAMAR has been working with the fishermen. Guy and Neca have hired those known to be good at finding eggs. The men have been adding to their income by taking eggs to TAMAR. Their children have been growing up with new ideas about turtles.

Two of these children, Flavio and Rosa, have always lived in Praia do Forte. Their father, Everaldo, is a fisherman who is very knowledgeable about turtles. He was one of the first men asked to find eggs for TAMAR.

Flavio and Rosa often roam the beach in their free time. They also like to visit their grandfather and hear about his life as a fisherman, about the time when there were plenty of turtle eggs to sell and eat. He tells the children how good the eggs tasted—and how he misses them.

After leaving their grandfather, the children go out to explore the beach for turtle nests. Flavio wears Grandfather's old hat. Most of the time the nests have been emptied by the oceanographers. But when Rosa sees the remains of a turtle's tracks, the children become excited. Perhaps this nest was made after the jeep finished its last tour of the night. They both begin to poke around in the sand.

Picking up a stick, Flavio and Rosa probe the sand the way their grandfather taught them. Sure enough, Rosa feels the stick slip into the egg cavity. They both begin to dig furiously, sending the sand flying in all directions.

Soon Flavio cannot reach any deeper, but Rosa, who is bigger, continues to dig. Stretching out her hand, she touches the leathery eggs and shouts with excitement. Then she hands the eggs to Flavio, who places them very carefully inside Grandfather's hat. When the hat is full, the children decide to stop and cover the rest of the eggs.

After covering the nest and marking the spot, Rosa and Flavio run to show their father the eggs. Along the way, they are joined by friends.

When Rosa and Flavio call out to him, their father appears over the side of the boat he is repairing. Flavio holds out the egg-filled hat. Everaldo is pleased that his children are also skilled at finding eggs. He tells them to show Guy and Neca what they have found. The children leave for the lighthouse.

The lighthouse is only a little way up the beach from the fishing boats. The area around it is fenced off. Inside the fence are rows of buried eggs that were found on the beaches. Each nest is surrounded by a mesh fence. There are also three large, round tanks where captive turtles are raised for study. Palm fronds shelter the tanks from the hot tropical sun.

The children are glad to have an excuse to visit the project. And Neca is delighted to see them and to receive the eggs.

Neca takes Rosa and Flavio to the rows of buried eggs. With a posthole digger, she makes a new hole. Rosa sticks her arm out to show Neca how deep the eggs were.

Just as the turtle did, Neca widens the base of the hole. She places the eggs in their new nest and covers them with sand. Then she takes a metal screen and forms a fence around the eggs, burying half of the fence in the sand.

Rosa and Flavio offer to take Neca to the nest where the rest of the eggs are. But before Neca can leave, she must note in a large book the number of eggs she has buried and the place where they were found. She must also assign the nest a number, which is painted on a stick and placed in the nest.

Flavio and Rosa climb into the back of the jeep. The children are thrilled to go for a ride. They bump along the coconut groves at the top of the beach until Rosa points out the site of the nest.

Once Neca has safely packed the rest of the eggs in a Styrofoam cooler and placed them in the jeep, she brings out a long white pole to mark the site of the empty nest. The pole has the same number as the one with the eggs she has buried—fourteen.

Neca tells the children that the eggs will hatch in about fifty days. At that time they can come to see their hatchlings.

Fifty days seems like such a long time to wait. Flavio and Rosa now make regular visits to the turtle pens. Often they wait for their father and the other fishermen to return from fishing. Sometimes little silver fish get stuck in the fishermen's nets. When the men shake out their nets on the beach, the children collect the little fish that fall out. These they take to the turtles in the tanks. Soon they have the turtles coming up to be fed.

Almost every night, while Rosa and Flavio are sleeping, turtles are hatching. Deep within the egg cavity, baby turtles break through their shells and, working together, burrow their way up through the sand. Soon the first tiny hatchling reaches the surface. It is then joined by dozens of little brothers and sisters.

Turtles prefer to hatch in the cool of the night.
They also enjoy the protection of the darkness,
which hides them from predators. During
the day their tiny black bodies would dry up on
the hot sand.

Now time is short. Once the hatchlings are
out of their shells, they must hurry to the
protective ocean. Neca and Alexandre count the
hatchlings, record the number, and place them
in a box.

Alexandre drives the hatchlings to the site of
their original nest, which is marked by a white
numbered pole. There he releases them onto the
sand. He wants them to experience the same
conditions they would have if they had hatched
there. Like little windup toys, their tiny flippers
flailing, the hatchlings climb over one another

and begin to scramble toward the sea. They are attracted by the luminous waves of the ocean. Alexandre helps them by standing in the shallow water with a flashlight.

Soon the hatchlings reach the white foamy edge of the surf. As they scurry to the safety of the ocean, wave after wave carries them away. When the last little hatchling is swallowed up by the sea, all that is left of them are the tiny tracks on the beach.

It has been fifty-three days since Flavio and Rosa found their eggs. That night Neca sticks her hand inside the nest and feels some movement. Sure enough, later in the night the hatchlings of pen number fourteen begin to emerge.

At dawn, Neca goes to fetch Flavio and Rosa. The children hurry to the pen to watch. As the

little baby turtles squirm and climb over one another, the children giggle with glee.

Now the sun is getting higher in the sky, and the heat of the day is beginning. Neca says they must hurry. They work together to load the hatchlings into a Styrofoam cooler.

In no time, the jeep takes them to pole number fourteen, the site of their original nest. Neca puts the box on its side, and the hatchlings make their way instinctively toward the ocean.

Thanks to Rosa and Flavio, who protect them from the birds, all the hatchlings complete their journey—all but one. Rosa picks up this last straggler. Gently she puts it down closer to the water. With the next wave the sea covers her hand, and the last of Rosa and Flavio's hatchlings is gone.

About

by George Ancona

Turtle Watch

Why did I do *Turtle Watch?* It wasn't so much the turtles, but rather the people whose lives are being affected by the turtle's scarcity, that prompted me to do the book. I had made friends of Brazilians who are concerned for their country, its forests, lands, ocean, and people. They told me about TAMAR, the government program to save the turtles. So I went to the tiny, remote fishing village of Praia do Forte (Beach of the Fort) in the north of Brazil, to meet and listen to the scientists, fisherfolk, and business people of the town. The biggest question in my mind was how the poor fishermen can be convinced to give up part of their meager income and not catch turtles or harvest their eggs. How can people with different needs work things out so they all can benefit?

In the ten days I spent in Praia do Forte I had my questions answered by

Neca and Guy, Julio and Alexandre, the scientists who introduced me to Rosa and Flavio and their family. We had lots of time to talk as each night we searched for turtles along the beaches. My plan was to spend ten days in the village. You can imagine my delight when we spotted a turtle on the first night out. She had just covered her nest and was on her way into the surf. Julio and Neca were able to examine, tag, and record her while I took pictures. Great! The first night out resulted in pictures. But now the important pictures I needed were those of a turtle laying her eggs. The next week became more and more frustrating. Each night we went out and returned without having sighted any more turtles. I had been told that there would be an abundance of turtles during this season. Yet each night was a disappointment. Time was running out and *no* turtles were laying eggs.

Finally, on the last night we spotted a turtle making her nest, and that's the one I was able to photograph for the book. I have watched my children being born and watching that turtle laying her eggs filled me with a similar awe and wonder at the miracle of life. After the turtle disappeared into the black waters we three stood for a while under the stars and stared out to sea.

Thinking

About

It

1. You are in this selection, *Turtle Watch*. You can be one of the people working for TAMAR, or you can be a fisherman, or you can be Flavio or Rosa. Who do you want to be? Why?

2. You've read about scientists who stay up all night to look for turtles laying eggs. You've seen them carefully pack the eggs in coolers. You've learned that the scientists pay people to bring them turtle eggs. Why are people so concerned about these turtles, anyway?

3. Which living things in your neighborhood need protection? Find out about them. What might you and your friends do to help?

THE GLITTERING CLOUD

from *On the Banks of Plum Creek*
by Laura Ingalls Wilder

Now the wheat was almost ready to cut. Every day Pa looked at it. Every night he talked about it, and showed Laura some long, stiff wheatheads. The plump grains were getting harder in their little husks. Pa said the weather was perfect for ripening wheat.

"If this keeps up," he said, "We'll start harvesting next week."

The weather was very hot. The thin, high sky was too hot to look at. Air rose up in waves from the whole prairie, as it does from a hot stove. In the schoolhouse the children panted like lizards, and the sticky pine-juice dripped down the board walls.

Saturday morning Laura went walking with Pa to look at the wheat. It was almost as tall as Pa. He lifted her onto his shoulder so that she could see over the heavy, bending tops. The field was greeny gold.

At the dinner table Pa told Ma about it. He had never seen such a crop. There were forty bushels to the acre, and wheat was a dollar a bushel. They were rich now. This was a wonderful country. Now they could have anything they wanted. Laura listened and thought, now Pa would get his new boots.

She sat facing the open door and the sunshine streaming through it. Something seemed to dim the sunshine. Laura rubbed her eyes and looked again. The sunshine really was dim. It grew dimmer until there was no sunshine.

"I do believe a storm is coming up," said Ma. "There must be a cloud over the sun."

Pa got up quickly and went to the door. A storm might hurt the wheat. He looked out, then he went out.

The light was queer. It was not like the changed light before a storm. The air did not press down as it did before a storm. Laura was frightened, she did not know why.

She ran outdoors, where Pa stood looking up at the sky. Ma and Mary came out, too, and Pa asked, "What do you make of that, Caroline?"

A cloud was over the sun. It was not like any cloud they had ever seen before. It was a cloud of something like snowflakes, but they were larger than snowflakes, and thin and glittering. Light shone through each flickering particle.

There was no wind. The grasses were still and the hot air did not stir, but the edge of the cloud came on across the sky faster than wind. The hair stood up on Jack's neck. All at once he made a frightful sound up at that cloud, a growl and a whine.

Plunk! something hit Laura's head and fell to the ground. She looked down and saw the largest grasshopper she had ever seen. Then huge brown grasshoppers were hitting the ground all around her, hitting her head and her face and her arms. They came thudding down like hail.

The cloud was hailing grasshoppers. The cloud *was* grasshoppers. Their bodies hid the sun and made darkness. Their thin, large wings gleamed and glittered. The rasping whirring of their wings filled the whole air and they hit the ground and the house with the noise of a hailstorm.

Laura tried to beat them off. Their claws clung to her skin and her dress. They looked at her with bulging eyes, turning their heads this way and that. Mary ran screaming into the house. Grasshoppers covered the ground, there was not one bare bit to step on. Laura had to step on grasshoppers and they smashed squirming and slimy under her feet.

Ma was slamming the windows shut, all around the house. Pa came and stood just inside the front door, looking out. Laura and Jack stood close beside him. Grasshoppers beat down from the sky and swarmed thick over the ground. Their long wings were folded and their strong legs took them hopping everywhere. The air whirred and the roof went on sounding like a roof in a hailstorm.

Then Laura heard another sound, one big sound made of tiny nips and snips and gnawings.

"The wheat!" Pa shouted. He dashed out the back door and ran toward the wheat-field.

The grasshoppers were eating. You could not hear one grasshopper eat, unless you listened very carefully while you held him and fed him grass. Millions and millions of grasshoppers were eating now. You could hear the millions of jaws biting and chewing.

Pa came running back to the stable. Through the window Laura saw him hitching Sam and David to the wagon. He began pitching old dirty hay from the manure-pile into the wagon, as fast as he could. Ma ran out, took the other pitchfork and helped him. Then he drove away to the wheat-field and Ma followed the wagon.

Pa drove around the field, throwing out little piles of stuff as he went. Ma stooped over one, then a thread of smoke rose from it and spread. Ma lighted pile after pile. Laura watched till a smudge of smoke hid the field and Ma and Pa and the wagon.

Grasshoppers were still falling from the sky. The light was still dim because grasshoppers covered the sun.

Ma came back to the house, and in the closed lean-to she took off her dress and her petticoats

and killed the grasshoppers she shook out of
them. She had lighted fires all around the
wheat-field. Perhaps smoke would keep the
grasshoppers from eating the wheat.

Ma and Mary and Laura were quiet in the
shut, smothery house. Carrie was so little that
she cried, even in Ma's arms. She cried herself to
sleep. Through the walls came the sound of
grasshoppers eating.

The darkness went away. The sun shone
again. All over the ground was a crawling,
hopping mass of grasshoppers. They were eating
all the soft, short grass off the knoll. The tall
prairie grasses swayed and bent and fell.

"Oh, look," Laura said, low, at the window.

They were eating the willow tops. The
willows' leaves were thin and bare twigs stuck
out. Then whole branches were bare, and knobby
with masses of grasshoppers.

"I don't want to look any more," Mary said,
and she went away from the window. Laura did

not want to look any more, either, but she could not stop looking.

The hens were funny. The two hens and their gawky pullets were eating grasshoppers with all their might. They were used to stretching their necks out low and running fast after grasshoppers and not catching them. Every time they stretched out now, they got a grasshopper right then. They were surprised. They kept stretching out their necks and trying to run in all directions at once.

"Well, we won't have to buy feed for the hens," said Ma. "There's no great loss without some gain."

The green garden rows were wilting down. The potatoes, the carrots, the beets and beans were being eaten away. The long leaves were eaten off the cornstalks, and the tassels, and the ears of young corn in their green husks fell covered with grasshoppers.

There was nothing anybody could do about it.

Smoke still hid the wheat-field. Sometimes Laura saw Pa moving dimly in it. He stirred up the smouldering fires and thick smoke hid him again.

When it was time to go for Spot, Laura put on stockings and shoes and a shawl. Spot was standing in the old ford of Plum Creek, shaking her skin and switching her tail. The herd went mournfully lowing beyond the old dugout. Laura was sure that cattle could not eat grass so full of grasshoppers. If the grasshoppers ate all the grass, the cattle would starve.

Grasshoppers were thick under her petticoats and on her dress and shawl. She kept striking them off her face and hands. Her shoes and Spot's feet crunched grasshoppers.

Ma came out in a shawl to do the milking. Laura helped her. They could not keep grasshoppers out of the milk. Ma had brought a cloth to cover the pail but they could not keep it covered while they milked into it. Ma skimmed out the grasshoppers with a tin cup.

Grasshoppers went into the house with them. Their clothes were full of grasshoppers. Some jumped onto the hot stove where Mary was starting supper. Ma covered the food till they had chased and smashed every grasshopper. She swept them up and shoveled them into the stove.

Pa came into the house long enough to eat supper while Sam and David were eating theirs. Ma did not ask him what was happening to the wheat. She only smiled and said: "Don't worry, Charles. We've always got along."

Pa's throat rasped and Ma said: "Have another cup of tea, Charles. It will help get the smoke out of your throat."

When Pa had drunk the tea, he went back to the wheat-field with another load of old hay and manure.

In bed, Laura and Mary could still hear the whirring and snipping and chewing. Laura felt claws crawling on her. There were no grass-hoppers in bed, but she could not brush the feeling off her arms and cheeks. In the dark she saw grasshoppers' bulging eyes and felt their claws crawling until she went to sleep.

Pa was not downstairs next morning. All night he had been working to keep the smoke over the wheat, and he did not come to breakfast. He was still working.

The whole prairie was changed. The grasses did not wave; they had fallen in ridges. The rising sun made all the prairie rough with shadows where the tall grasses had sunk against each other.

The willow trees were bare. In the plum thickets only a few plum pits hung to the leafless branches. The nipping, clicking, gnawing sound of the grasshoppers' eating was still going on.

At noon Pa came driving the wagon out of the smoke. He put Sam and David into the stable, and slowly came to the house. His face was black with smoke and his eyeballs were red. He hung his hat on the nail behind the door and sat down at the table.

"It's no use, Caroline," he said. "Smoke won't stop them. They keep dropping down through it and hopping in from all sides. The wheat is falling now. They're cutting it off like a scythe. And eating it, straw and all."

He put his elbows on the table and hid his face with his hands. Laura and Mary sat still. Only Carrie on her high stool rattled her spoon and reached her little hand toward the bread. She was too young to understand.

"Never mind, Charles," Ma said. "We've been through hard times before."

Laura looked down at Pa's patched boots under the table and her throat swelled and ached. Pa could not have new boots now.

Pa's hands came down from his face and he picked up his knife and fork. His beard smiled, but his eyes would not twinkle. They were dull and dim.

"Don't worry, Caroline," he said. "We did all we could, and we'll pull through somehow."

Then Laura remembered that the new house was not paid for. Pa had said he would pay for it when he harvested the wheat.

It was a quiet meal, and when it was over Pa lay down on the floor and went to sleep. Ma slipped a pillow under his head and laid her finger on her lips to tell Laura and Mary to be still.

They took Carrie into the bedroom and kept her quiet with their paper dolls. The only sound was the sound of the grasshoppers' eating.

Day after day the grasshoppers kept on eating. They ate all the wheat and the oats. They ate every green thing—all the garden and all the prairie grass.

"Oh, Pa, what will the rabbits do?" Laura asked. "And the poor birds?"

"Look around you, Laura," Pa said.

The rabbits had all gone away. The little birds of the grass tops were gone. The birds that were left were eating grasshoppers. And prairie hens ran with outstretched necks, gobbling grasshoppers.

When Sunday came, Pa and Laura and Mary walked to Sunday school. The sun shone so bright and hot that Ma said she would stay at home with Carrie, and Pa left Sam and David in the shady stable.

There had been no rain for so long that Laura walked across Plum Creek on dry stones. The whole prairie was bare and brown. Millions of brown grasshoppers whirred low over it. Not a green thing was in sight anywhere.

All the way, Laura and Mary brushed off grasshoppers. When they came to the church, brown grasshoppers were thick on their petticoats. They lifted their skirts and brushed them off before they went in. But careful as they were, the grasshoppers had spit tobacco-juice on their best Sunday dresses.

Nothing would take out the horrid stains. They would have to wear their best dresses with the brown spots on them.

Many people in town were going back East. Christy and Cassie had to go. Laura said good-bye to Christy and Mary said good-bye to Cassie, their best friends.

They did not go to school any more. They must save their shoes for winter and they could not bear to walk barefooted on grasshoppers. School would be ended soon, anyway, and Ma said she would teach them through the winter so they would not be behind their classes when school opened again next spring.

Pa worked for Mr. Nelson and earned the use of Mr. Nelson's plough. He began to plough the bare wheat-field, to make it ready for next year's wheat crop.

THINKING ABOUT IT

1

Is there anything you'd like to change in "The Glittering Cloud"? Which parts would you change, or would you keep the story exactly the same? Why?

2

Author Laura Ingalls Wilder was especially good at describing settings and action. Find a scene or description in the story that you can picture in your mind almost as clearly as if it were real.

3

Your company, Grasshopper-Be-Gone, Inc., promises to get rid of the Ingalls family's grasshopper problem. How will you do it?

ALL ALONE

from *Addie Across the Prairie*
by Laurie Lawlor

In this story it is 1883. Ten-year-old Addie Mills is traveling with her family from their home in Sabula, Iowa, a town on the Mississippi River, to their 160-acre homestead in Oak Hollow, Dakota Territory. Addie's family didn't want to leave Iowa and their relatives and friends, but it was a chance for them, as it was for many people in those days, to own their own land.

The five-hundred-mile trip has taken several weeks. Winter is coming when they arrive in Dakota, and the first thing they have to do is build a sod house. Building a "soddy" is hard work, and Addie's family needs the help of their friends, Mr. and Mrs. Fency, with whom they are staying. While both families are off working on the soddy, Addie is left in charge of the Fency's farm and her two-year-old brother, Burt, for two days.

In the early morning darkness, Addie watched the two wagons until they disappeared on the northwestern horizon. Her family had taken all their supplies, Big Jones, and the oxen, which would be needed to pull the breaking plow through the tough sod. From the soddy roof, Addie waved her sunbonnet over and over again, straining her eyes to see a glimmer of white, some other sunbonnet—maybe Anna's or her mother's. Maybe if she tried hard enough, she could make out Mr. Fency's tall shape. In a few minutes they would all be out of sight. Addie sighed. Already she missed them—everyone, of course, except George. She didn't care if she never saw him again.

When every trace of her family and the Fencys was gone, Addie remained on the roof for a long time, watching the place where they had disappeared. She reminded herself of what Pa had said about being resourceful. She knew she could take care of Burt and the cows and chickens. And she certainly no longer feared Indians the way she once had. But it was the thought of spending the night alone that troubled her. The prairie was so black, even when there were stars and a moon. There were no neighbors' lights nearby, the way there had been in Sabula. She would be alone with Burt in a house without a door, listening to the terrible howling of the wolves.

"Eleanor was right. I *am* a fraidycat," Addie said to Ruby Lillian. Her smile did not seem reassuring today.

Addie climbed down off the roof and went inside to nibble on a cold biscuit and butter. She checked her brother, who was still sleeping, then she filled a bowl with some of the oatmeal Anna had left on the back of the stove. She propped her doll on the table against a tin cup as she ate breakfast. "Now Ruby Lillian, remember what I told you." Addie imitated the voice of Mr. Fency. "Milk the cows, give them fresh hay and water, strain the milk, and carry the milk pans to the root cellar to let the cream rise. Feed the chickens and gather the eggs. Watch Burt so he doesn't wander too close to the well or tip over a lighted dish of tallow. Don't let the fire go out, and be sure you skim the cream from the milk when it's cool. Can you remember all that, Ruby Lillian?"

When she had finished her breakfast, Addie sat at the table, drumming her fingers. Even with all the chores, it was still going to be a long day. Mother had left her a sampler to practice her stitches on. And there were always more cats to twist, but right now Addie did not feel like doing much of anything—not even cleaning up her breakfast dishes.

"And don't forget to sweep up the old grass from the soddy and lay down some new dried grass on the floor," she reminded Ruby Lillian, picking up the broom made of stiff hay bound to the end of a stick. With a sigh, Addie began sweeping. Building a new house seemed much more exciting than staying behind and taking care of Burt. If there were someone here like

Eleanor to talk to, at least then the time might pass more quickly.

As she swept, Addie had an idea. She turned the broom upside down and put her bonnet on the stiff bristles. She tied the bonnet, wrapped an apron around the broom handle, and leaned the broom against the table.

"So nice of you to join us this morning," she said to her new companion. "Miss Primrose, please meet Miss Ruby Lillian."

The broom in the sunbonnet was very polite but rather shy. Nonetheless, Addie was pleased that Miss Primrose and Ruby Lillian seemed to get along so well, especially since this was the first time they'd met. "Would you care for tea or coffee?" Addie said, placing two tin cups on the table. "I'm sorry I can only offer you sugar. We have no lemons this time of year," she apologized, using the same words she remembered her mother saying when the minister came

to call last spring. Addie imagined Miss Primrose nodding politely and sipping her tea. "You know the price of store-bought sugar is very dear these days," she added. She waited for Miss Primrose to answer.

When she couldn't think of anything for Miss Primrose to say, Addie sat down at the table with her chin in her hands. She wished her brother would wake up so that there'd be someone real to talk to. She was beginning to feel a little nervous all by herself. She touched the Indian necklace around her neck. Maybe she wasn't brave enough to wear a special eagle feather. She hesitated for a moment but decided to keep the necklace on after all. Maybe she would feel braver if she were busy. "After all, it *is* time to milk the cows," she reminded herself and went to the lean-to with a metal bucket.

Bess and Missy seemed to look at her in surprise as she sat down on the Fencys' milking

stool. The smell of sweet grass and warm cows filled the little shed, making Addie feel safe and comfortable. She had been milking cows since she was six, and it was a chore she knew how to do very well. Little by little the metal bucket filled, ringing with a tinny sound as the spray of milk hit its sides. When she was done, Addie carried the milk to the soddy and strained it carefully with a sieve into pans. She lifted the trap door in one corner of the soddy's floor. This led to the root cellar, a hole that extended under the lean-to.

She placed a dish of tallow with a rag lit in it near the edge of the trap-door opening, just as she had seen Anna do. Then she stepped down the short ladder into the cellar, carrying one pan of milk at a time. The root cellar was four feet deep, large enough for the Fencys to store two or three barrels and several bushel baskets and wooden boxes of food. In the boxes were carrots covered with sand, crocks of cooked pork sealed with lard, dried corn, and jars of canned cabbage, plums, green beans, tomatoes, and watermelon pickles. Cabbage heads hung from the ceiling by their roots. The root cellar was dark and cool, and Addie did not like to stay down there long because of the way the tallow light threw shadows on the walls. She set the pans of milk on top of a barrel and hurried back up the ladder. Quickly she replaced the trap door and went outside to give the cows fresh hay and water.

When Burt woke up, Addie gave him a bowl of oatmeal with plenty of corn sweetener.

"Mama?" he asked, pounding the table with his sticky spoon.

"Mama will be back soon," Addie said, dabbing a corner of her apron with water and wiping oatmeal from her brother's hair. "You look a mess, Burt." She pulled his damp flannel shirt-dress over his head and put a clean one on him. She didn't want Burt to get sick with the croup from wearing wet clothes.

Her brother watched her while she rinsed the little shirt and rubbed it with soap against the washboard. He followed her outside as she carried the basket of damp laundry Anna had washed the night before. When she was finished hanging everything on the line, Burt helped his sister search for eggs in the tall grass around the soddy. While they were looking, Addie found a spiderweb delicately stretched between some butterfly milkweeds and the dried stalk of a sunflower. Droplets of dew clung to the web and shimmered in the morning light. She and Eleanor had called these "fairy necklaces" whenever they found them in the forest near the Mills's farm in Jackson County. "Pretty, isn't it?" Addie asked Burt. Her brother didn't seem interested. He was waving a stick at a chicken. Addie wished Eleanor were here to share the sight of the fairy necklace with her.

Addie went back inside and greased the two eggs she had found with lard the way Anna had showed her. She buried them in the barrel filled with grain in the root cellar. "The cows have been fed, the floor swept," she said looking to

Miss Primrose for approval. "How am I doing?"

Addie spent the rest of the morning outside, building a little castle of stones and sticks for Ruby Lillian and Burt. She had seen a castle in one of Eleanor's books. The parts of the castle she couldn't remember, she just made up. Little by little the building grew in a patch of bare, dry ground outside the soddy.

It was a bright, warm Indian summer day. Because the weather was so pleasant, they ate a picnic lunch of biscuits and cheese near the new castle. "Careful, Burt, don't knock it down just yet," she told her brother as she carefully placed a flag of dry Indian grass between two stones. "Oh, Burt! Now see what you've done!" Addie cried, rescuing Ruby Lillian from underneath a fallen castle wall.

Burt sheepishly removed his foot from the center of the castle. His bottom lip trembled as he stared at the ruins. He looked as if he might begin crying at any moment. Before he had a chance, Addie let out a wild whoop and gathered him in her arms. With Burt slung over her shoulder, she galloped out past the firebreak until he laughed and laughed.

In the evening Addie finished the last of the day's chores. She skimmed the cream from the milk in the root cellar and made a dinner of pearled barley cooked in buttermilk. "Tomorrow we'll go looking for prairie dog houses," she told her brother as she smoothed his hair and pulled his quilt over his shoulders. At least she had Burt for company, she thought.

Addie lit a piece of rag in a dish of tallow and set this on the table. Then she made sure the canvas flaps at the door and window were pulled tight to keep the prairie night out. She took out her sampler and began practicing the stitches her mother had taught her. Addie worked one row of cross-stitch that was a border for the alphabet.

"How do you like my cross-stitch, Ruby Lillian? Or do you think my running stitch is better?" Addie asked. Ruby Lillian smiled from her perch atop the wooden cracker box but remained silent. Addie sighed. What fun were friends if they couldn't say anything?

It was hard to make the stitches even in the dim light. She put the sampler away and opened Anna's trunk. Anna had told her she could read the books if she were careful Burt didn't touch them. She admired the beautiful color pictures in *Aesop's Fables*. It seemed a luxury to read without being interrupted by anyone. But somehow tonight not even the tortoise and the hare could make her forget that she and Burt were all alone.

Burt snored loudly and uncurled from a tight ball. Addie listened hard. Beyond the walls of the soddy, beyond the flimsy canvas covering the doorway and the window, she could hear it beginning, the sound she had been dreading. The wolves were howling. She covered her ears with her hands, but the mournful sound would not go away.

Addie placed a few more twisted cats into the fire. She left the rag light burning on the table and pushed Anna's trunk and a nail keg against the doorway. Then she kicked off her shoes and tucked Ruby Lillian under her pillow. She took up Anna's heavy rolling pin and crawled in under the covers next to Burt. She didn't even bother to change into her nightclothes. If the wolves came, she would be ready to defend herself and her brother with the only weapon left in the house—the rolling pin. More than ever she wished that Pa had taught her how to shoot. If only he hadn't taken the gun!

Addie pulled the quilt up over her ears and waited for sleep to come, clutching the rolling pin in one hand. Instead of sleeping, she could only stare at the shadows on the flap over the doorway. She shut her eyes and listened to her brother snore. Nothing seemed to be frightening him. Addie began counting his snores and little by little felt herself growing drowsy.

The next thing she knew she was waking up, and there was light coming in around the edges of the canvas at the window. She had survived the night alone. She sat up and stretched. The

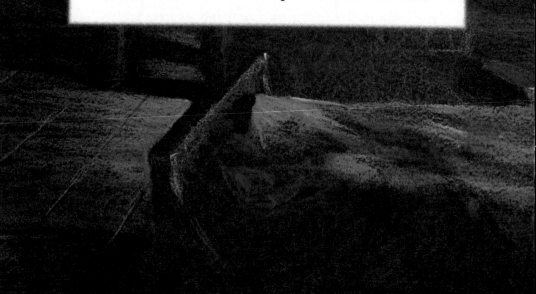

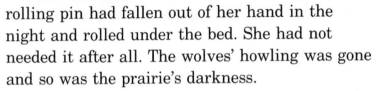

rolling pin had fallen out of her hand in the night and rolled under the bed. She had not needed it after all. The wolves' howling was gone and so was the prairie's darkness.

Quietly, so as not to wake Burt, she climbed out of bed and splashed her face with a handful of water from the bucket. She threw more cats into the stove and filled a kettle with water to make tea. Then she went outside. The morning air felt cold and she could see her breath in little white puffs. But there was no frost, only dew clinging to the dried grass.

When Addie had finished the milking and her other morning chores, she prepared a breakfast of gruel for herself and Burt. Carefully she dropped pinches of cornmeal into the boiling water. She felt pleased about how well she was doing on her own.

"Don't you think I'm doing just fine?" she asked Ruby Lillian, as she took her out from beneath the pillow and placed her on the table. Addie spooned gruel into two bowls.

"Mama! Mama!" Burt demanded.

"She'll be back, Burt. Pa's coming to get us soon as he can." Addie sighed. It still seemed like a long, long time to wait for her parents to return. But she had made it through the night. The worst was over.

She washed her breakfast dishes, swept, read Burt a story from Anna's book, and then took him outside to look for prairie dogs.

In the afternoon while Burt napped, Addie worked on her sampler again. Suddenly she heard low bellows from the cows. What was the matter with Bess and Missy? A gust of wind blew into the soddy, knocking the canvas flap against the wall. Addie looked outside. The sky seemed unusually dark for this time of the afternoon. Or had she lost track of time? Was it later than she thought?

The wind blew dust through the yard, and the cows continued making frightened noises. Addie hurried to the clothesline to make sure the laundry she had forgotten on the line since yesterday had not blown away. She gathered the bedding and Burt's clothes. Pulling the flapping sheets away from her face, she saw a queer sight in the southwestern sky. The far horizon was ablaze with orange and yellow, as if the sun were setting.

But Addie knew exactly where the sun set. She had watched the western horizon every day since they left Iowa. This glow wasn't from the sun.

She bundled the laundry together and tossed it inside the soddy, then scrambled up the ladder to the roof for a better look. As she climbed, the wind grew stronger. She crawled along the roof, shielding her eyes from flying dust and sharp pieces of brittle grass. A family of coyotes raced through Mr. Fency's plowed field, not even stopping to bother Anna's chickens, who frantically clucked near the lean-to. Addie wiped her eyes with her apron and discovered that her face was covered with black flecks. There were cinders flying in the air! The bright glow she saw was a prairie fire, and it was headed right for the Fency farm.

The palms of her hands broke into a cold sweat. She had to think of a way to save herself and Burt. She had to think of a way to save the farm. She scrambled off the roof and ran inside the soddy to wake her brother.

"Burt! Wake up!" she screamed. "We've got to get out of here!"

Burt's eyes flew open, and he began to whimper. He knew something was terribly wrong as he watched his sister gather Anna's books and stuff them back into the trunk. With all her strength she pushed the trunk across the room and opened the trap door to the root cellar. She shoved the trunk into the cellar with one terrific push. There was barely enough room for it. Neither she nor Burt would fit down there as well. She slammed the door.

"Where are we going to hide? What are we going to do?" she blurted and ran outside. The wind swept across the yard, picking up dried leaves and pieces of grass and sending them into the sky in little corkscrew formations. Addie remembered what Pa had said about a stiff wind behind a prairie fire. Would the Fencys' firebreak save them? The cows were bellowing in terror now. Addie decided to untie Bess and Missy and let them run from the fire. Their eyes rolled as they pulled against their ropes. "Run as fast as you can!" Addie shouted, hitting each cow on the rump. Should she and Burt try to run too? But how far could they get in bare feet?

Addie raced back into the soddy and put on her black, copper-toed boots. She quickly slipped Burt's shoes on him. Pulling him by the hand, she ran outside again. They were past the firebreak, running away from the fire as fast as

Addie could go, when she realized she had left Ruby Lillian behind on the table. She picked Burt up and dashed back. The soddy's darkness and quiet made the fire seem farther away. She wanted to stay there, but she knew she couldn't. From the door she could see that the approaching flames were as tall as three houses stacked one atop the other. The wind was so strong the firebreak would never work. She knew there wasn't time to set a backfire, even if she knew how.

"A fire can't go where there's nothing to burn." Addie repeated Pa's words frantically, trying to think of a plan. She crouched and motioned to her brother. "Get on my back, Burt." The child sobbed tearfully but did as he was told.

She ran outside with Burt on her back and Ruby Lillian in her pocket. The wall of fire was closer; she could see tufts of grass exploding into flames. With each explosion the sky filled with more and more billows of black smoke. The roar was deafening, like a terrible, rolling summer thunderstorm.

"I promised to watch the farm and keep it safe," she told Burt, placing him on the ground near the well. "I can't let the Fencys' house burn." She lowered bucket after bucket into the water, soaking the soddy's walls as best she could. But even as she desperately tossed water, more pieces of burning grass landed on the roof. Saving the soddy seemed hopeless. Addie pulled the ladder away from the house and threw it on the ground just as it was about to catch fire too.

She would never be able to keep the house from burning all by herself.

Addie was exhausted, but she kept hauling bucket after bucket up the well as best she could. She could not think. Her arms kept working as if she had no control over them. As she pulled up one more bucket, she saw her reflection in the water, illuminated by the fire's glow. She and Burt had only a few minutes before the sea of flames would engulf them. Where could she find a place to hide from those awful, devouring explosions? "Where's there nothing to burn," Addie whispered. Suddenly she knew what to do. She dragged the ladder to the well, the way she had done to save her doll, Eleanor. She pushed it down inside.

Burt was crying hysterically, crouched on the ground with his hands over his ears to stop the horrible noise. "Come on, Burt, we have to hurry. Climb on my back," Addie shouted.

"No, NO!" Burt sobbed.

"You have to!" Addie commanded. She knelt beside her brother. Reluctantly he grabbed around her shoulders, crying harder than ever.

Still kneeling on the ground, Addie used one foot to carefully feel for the ladder's highest rung. Slowly, she lowered herself, balancing Burt with great effort. Down into the well she went, step over step. Now they were below ground level. It was pitch black, and the water felt cold around Addie's knees as she reached the bottom rung. "Don't let go, Burt. Don't let go," she told her brother, who buried his face into the back of her neck so that her necklace dug deep into her skin.

The terrible roar of the fire grew louder. Addie wanted to cover both her ears, but she could not let go. She had to hold on tight to the ladder while standing as still as possible. Any minute the fire would be right over them. What would happen then. Would they melt? She remained motionless even as several stones and a handful of dirt came loose from the wall and tumbled into the water. Was the well going to cave in on them?

Now the noise was deafening. Pieces of burning grass hissed as they fell into the well water, just missing the children. Cinders smarted Addie's eyes. How long? How long until the fire came? Addie glanced up just as the flames roared over the mouth of the well.

Addie held her breath and closed her eyes. For one brief, horrible moment she was certain her hair would catch fire. The hot white light charged overhead with a howling ten times worse than the loudest locomotive Addie had ever heard. But as quickly as the flames appeared, they were gone.

A gust of wind blew more cinders and smoke into the well, and the children began coughing. Around the edge of the well, where Mr. Fency had laid sod bricks, Addie could see a few small flames sputter and go out as the last piece of dry grass was consumed.

"Burt? Are you all right?" she asked in a hoarse whisper.

"Mama! Mama!" his voice echoed in the well. He clung to Addie even more tightly.

Her legs shook in the cold water. A terrible pain shot up and down her back where her brother dug in with his knees. But still she did not move or change position. She felt as if she were frozen, clinging to the ladder for dear life. Nearly half an hour passed. There was no more roar to be heard, even in the distance, and the air seemed filled with an almost eerie silence.

Addie whispered again, "Burt, are you all right? I'm going to climb back up now. Don't touch the walls. Don't touch anything. Just hold on tight to me."

Addie climbed up one step. Then another. She stopped as some rocks tumbled past and splashed in the water. Burt whimpered and coughed. The top of the well seemed almost farther than Addie could manage. She was exhausted. Burt felt heavier by the minute, even though he weighed only a bit more than twenty-five pounds. If only Pa would come now and lift them both out. If only he would save them.

"Addie!" Burt cried, his voice echoing. "Out! Out!"

"Hush, Burt!" Addie hissed as a small section of the well wall crumbled and collapsed above them, sending dirt all over their faces and hair.

Pa wasn't going to save them. The only way they could get out was if she climbed out herself, with Burt on her back. Somehow she'd just have to trust that she could make it all nine feet up to the top. "Hold on, Burt. We're almost there," she said, her voice cracking. Only four more steps.

Suddenly Addie heard a familiar voice.

"Addie! Addie! Where are you?" someone called desperately.

It wasn't Pa. It was George!

"We're in the well!" Addie shouted. Another pile of dirt splashed into the water.

A face peered down at her. "Grab hold of my hand," George said, throwing his coat over the charred sod at the well's edge and lying on his stomach, his arms reaching down to them. "Careful now. Not too fast."

The ladder teetered as she reached the top-most rung. Addie made a desperate lunge for George's hands and solid ground. As her foot left the top rung, one side of the wall began to crumble. A section of stones and dirt broke loose and crashed into the water. Addie threw herself forward, grasped the well's edge with both hands, and scrambled to safe ground. Burt tumbled from her back, unharmed.

Addie hugged George as Burt jumped up and down with excitement. She couldn't believe how happy she was to see him. Her brother seemed just as happy to see her.

"You should take a look at yourself, Addie," George said, grinning. "Your face is black as a skunk's. Yours too, Burt. Mother will hardly recognize you."

"Pa and Mother are all right? What about the others? You didn't get caught in the fire?" Addie asked anxiously.

"The fire passed to the south of us, heading straight east on the other side of the river. We were on our way back when we saw it coming. We headed to get you two as fast as we could travel. I rode ahead of the others to look for you.

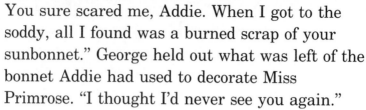

You sure scared me, Addie. When I got to the soddy, all I found was a burned scrap of your sunbonnet." George held out what was left of the bonnet Addie had used to decorate Miss Primrose. "I thought I'd never see you again."

"You won't get rid of me that easily, George Sidney," Addie said. She looked sheepishly at the toes of her dirty, wet boots. "I'm sorry about what I said to you before you left. I don't really hate you."

George blushed. "You aren't a crybaby, either. I just said that to be mean. You're about the bravest person I know. I don't believe I'd have been able to figure what to do if I'd gotten caught in a prairie fire."

"You really think I'm brave?" Addie asked, suddenly feeling wonderful in spite of her damp clothes and aching back. "But you know, George, I *was* afraid down there." She hestitated. "And I was afraid when the Indians came here too."

"Maybe you were scared, but you did something courageous anyway. I think that's what being brave's all about."

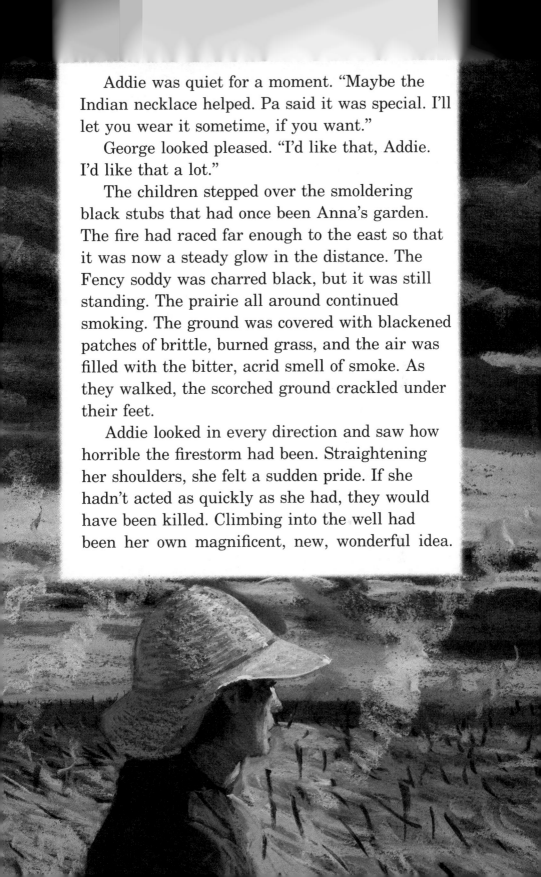

Addie was quiet for a moment. "Maybe the Indian necklace helped. Pa said it was special. I'll let you wear it sometime, if you want."

George looked pleased. "I'd like that, Addie. I'd like that a lot."

The children stepped over the smoldering black stubs that had once been Anna's garden. The fire had raced far enough to the east so that it was now a steady glow in the distance. The Fency soddy was charred black, but it was still standing. The prairie all around continued smoking. The ground was covered with blackened patches of brittle, burned grass, and the air was filled with the bitter, acrid smell of smoke. As they walked, the scorched ground crackled under their feet.

Addie looked in every direction and saw how horrible the firestorm had been. Straightening her shoulders, she felt a sudden pride. If she hadn't acted as quickly as she had, they would have been killed. Climbing into the well had been her own magnificent, new, wonderful idea.

She had been very brave, just as George had said. She had saved her brother and herself. That was something, wasn't it? She had survived an Indian visit all alone too. Dakota didn't seem quite so frightening anymore. Maybe Eleanor was wrong. Maybe she *was* a sodbusting pioneer-type after all.

The wagon and horses rumbled into what was left of the Fencys' yard, and Pa and Mother leapt quickly to the ground.

"Lord be praised! Lord be praised!" Mother kept saying, hugging the children and kissing their faces over and over as if she couldn't believe they were really there. "Are you all right? How did you manage to get through that fire alive? It came up so fast! If I'd thought anything so terrible could have happened, I never would have left you here alone. Never!" She burst into tears, and that was the second time Addie had ever seen her mother cry.

"Found them in the well, Mother," George said, awkwardly patting his mother's shoulder. "They were standing on the ladder."

"So you climbed into the well, Addie. That was a wise thing to do, a very wise thing. If you'd gone anywhere else, I just . . . I just don't know," Pa said in a broken voice, gathering Addie up in his arms even though she was much too big to be carried. "You saved your brother's life as well as your own. The firebreak couldn't hold off those flames. The wind was too strong."

Anna had gone inside the soddy, and Mr. Fency was poking about the yard and the lean-to, trying to see what was left. He came over to Addie and her family, his shoulders stooped. He did not look as tall as he once had. "Fire was so hot, it melted my plow handles. My seed for next year's planting is gone. I found the carcasses of Bess and Missy. The house is still standing, but everything inside was destroyed."

"I let the cows go. It was my fault," said Addie sadly. "I thought they'd have a better chance running away from the fire."

"You did the best thing, little sister," Mr. Fency said slowly. "The firebreak couldn't have held up against a fire moving that fast. And there's no way you could have gotten the cows down inside the well. I'm only glad you and Burt are safe."

"Addie's a plucky little gal," Pa said. "Mr. Fency, you and Anna can come back with us. We'll finish our soddy while things cool off here. Then George and I will help you get settled again. In the spring you can use my plow and some of my seed. I've got more than enough."

From the house came a moan, and Anna appeared, her eyes red from crying. "Everything inside's destroyed, even my trunk. All my fine things burned. Everything I brought from Michigan—all our photographs, our winter clothing, our bedding and linens. Things I've had since we were first married. Everything's gone." She wiped her eyes with her apron. Mother put her arm around Anna.

Addie slipped away, feeling as though it were all her fault that she hadn't been able to save

any of the Fencys' things. What had happened to
the trunk? She entered the smoke-filled soddy
and kicked away the burned grass and the
remains of the Fencys' table and bed. She found
the trap door to the root cellar. It was so charred
that when she kicked hard, it fell apart.

"Anna! Mr. Fency!" Addie called as she stuck
her head down into the root cellar.

With help from Pa, Mr. Fency lifted the big
trunk out of the root cellar and carried it into the
yard. Anna opened it and stared in disbelief.
Everything inside was safe.

"And the provisions we stored in the cellar
aren't touched either," Mr. Fency said, his face
beaming.

"You still have Ruby Lillian too," Addie said.
She reached in her pocket and carefully placed
Ruby Lillian in Anna's hand.

Again, Anna's eyes filled with tears as she
turned the doll over and over in her hands.
"Thanks to you, Addie, I have much, much more.
I have you and Burt." She put her arms around
Addie. "If we'd all been here when that fire
came, we never would have all fit in that well,
that's for certain. Who knows if any of us would
have survived? You keep Ruby Lillian for me,
will you? You saved her life too."

Pulling It All Together

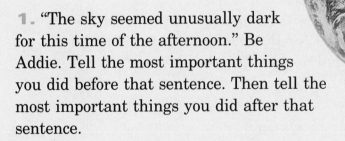

1. "The sky seemed unusually dark for this time of the afternoon." Be Addie. Tell the most important things you did before that sentence. Then tell the most important things you did after that sentence.

2. Think of all the characters you met in the selections in *Y.O.U.* Which one would you like to get to know better? Why?

3. You've read about friends, places, and animals—all important parts of your universe. What are some other parts of your universe? Which ones would you like to read about?

Books to Enjoy

Little House on the Prairie
by Laura Ingalls Wilder

Laura and her family help one another as they get used to life on the prairie.

Along Came a Dog
by Meindert De Jong
illustrations by Maurice Sendak

A big black dog longs to become part of a barnyard family. But all he finds at first is a little red hen and a lot of trouble.

Atuk
by Mischa Damjan
illustrations by Jozef Wilkon

Atuk loves his little brown sled dog, Taruk. He dreams that someday they will lead their own team. When Taruk is attacked by a wolf, Atuk learns to turn his hate for the wolf into love.

Santiago
by Pura Belpre
illustrations by Symeon Shimin

Santiago lives in New York City but dreams of his past in Puerto Rico. He is upset when friends don't believe all his stories from the past.

The Wild Horses of Sweetbriar
by Natalie Kinsey-Warnock

The author recalls the terrible winter of 1903 when she took care of a herd of wild horses off the coast of Nantucket.

Peeping in the Shell: A Whooping Crane is Hatched
by Faith McNulty

The endangered whooping crane has a safe place to live in Wisconsin. See why people spend their lives watching over these unusual birds.

Appalachia: The Voices of Sleeping Birds
by Cynthia Rylant
Illustrations by Barry Moser

What is growing up in Appalachia like? Read about the closeness these people feel to nature, their families, and their pets.

John and the Fiddler
by Patricia Foley

An old violin maker teaches a young boy about the beauty of music, friendship, and the value of a parting gift.

Literary Terms

Exaggeration

Exaggeration, overstating something or making it seem more dramatic than it really is, often adds to the humor in a story. In "Fitting In," from *The Kid in the Red Jacket,* Howard describes drinking so much water that his stomach sloshes. He calls the playground supervisor Rambo, and says that he was so lonely he would have paid someone to eat lunch with him. These exaggerated statements keep readers smiling as they read the story.

Figurative Language

Figurative language describes one thing in terms of another. Metaphor and simile are two kinds of figurative language. In "The Glittering Cloud," grasshoppers are described as a cloud of something like snowflakes. In another part of the story, the author writes that the cloud was hailing grasshoppers and that grasshoppers were falling from the sky. Describing the grasshoppers like hail falling from the sky helps readers picture just what the grasshoppers looked like and how they could destroy crops.

Historical Fiction

Realistic stories set in the past are **historical fiction.** You can learn quite a bit about past times from the details in historical fictional books. "The Glittering Cloud" from *On the Banks of Plum Creek* and "All Alone" from *Addie Across the Prairie* are both historical fiction. What are some things you learned about life on the prairie long ago from these two pieces?

Imagery

Images are words that appeal to the senses. They help the reader experience the way things look, sound, smell, taste, or feel. Think about "Early Spring." Do you see something when you read the poem? hear something? feel something?

Rhyme

Rhyme is the repetition of sounds in at least the last syllable of two or more words. "Cat" and "hat" rhyme because they have the same ending sound. Some poems rhyme and some don't. "Two Friends" and "Winter Poem" do not rhyme.

Glossary

Vocabulary from your selections

a·cre (ā′kər), a unit of area
equal to 160 square rods or
43,560 square feet. *noun.*

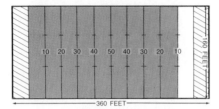

acre—An **acre** is smaller than a
football field. The green part of this
football field is an **acre.**

ap·pre·ci·ate (ə prē′shē āt), **1** to
think highly of; recognize the
worth or quality of; value;
enjoy. **2** to be thankful for.
verb, **ap·pre·ci·ates,
ap·pre·ci·at·ed, ap·pre·ci·at·ing.**

ar·gue (är′gyü), **1** to discuss
with someone who disagrees.
2 to give reasons for or against
something. *verb,* **ar·gues,
ar·gued, ar·gu·ing.**

au·to·mat·ic (ô′tə mat′ik),
1 able to work by itself. **2** done
without thought or attention.
adjective.

au·to·mat·i·cal·ly (ô′tə mat′ik
lē), in an automatic manner;
unthinkingly. *adverb.*

coax (kōks), to persuade by soft
words; influence by pleasant
ways. *verb.*

co·in·ci·dence (kō in′sə dəns),
the happening by chance of
two things at the same time or
place in such a way as to seem
remarkable or planned. *noun.*

con·cert (kon′sərt), a musical
performance in which one or
more musicians take part: *The
orchestra gave a concert. noun.*

con·ser·va·tion·ist (kon′sər vā′
shə nist), a person who wants
to preserve and protect the
forests and other natural
resources of a country. *noun.*

con·trac·tion (kən trak′shən),
1 a shrinking; drawing
together. **2** something
contracted; a shortened form:
*"Can't" is a contraction of
"cannot." noun.*

deaf·en (def′ən), to make deaf,
especially for a short time.
verb. **deaf·ens, deaf·ened,
deaf·en·ing.**

den (den), **1** a wild animal's
home or resting place. **2** a
private room for reading and
work, usually small and cozy.
noun.

des·per·ate (des′pər it), **1** not
caring what happens because
hope is gone. **2** ready to try
anything; ready to run any
risk. **3** having little chance for
hope or cure. *adjective.*

des·per·ate·ly (des′pər it lē), in
a desperate or frantic manner.
adverb. See **desperate.**

di·gest (də jest′), **1** to change food in the stomach and intestines, so that the body can use it. **2** to think over something until it becomes a part of your own thought. *verb.*

a	hat	i	it	oi	oil	ch	child	ə stands for:
ā	age	ī	ice	ou	out	ng	long	a in about
ä	far	o	hot	u	cup	sh	she	e in taken
e	let	ō	open	ù	put	th	thin	i in pencil
ē	equal	ô	order	ü	rule	ŦH	then	o in lemon
ėr	term					zh	measure	u in circus

e·merge (i mėrj′), to come out; come up; come into view: *The sun emerged from behind a cloud. verb,* **e·merg·es, e·merged, e·merg·ing.**

en·gulf (en gulf′), to swallow up; overwhelm. *verb.*

fine (fīn), **1** a sum of money paid as a punishment for breaking a law or regulation. **2** to make pay such a sum. 1 *noun,* 2 *verb,* **fines, fined, fin·ing.**

flick·er (flik′ər), to shine or burn with an unsteady, wavering light: *The firelight flickered on the walls. verb.*

fran·ti·cal·ly (fran′tik lē), in a frantic manner; with wild excitement. *adverb.*

grass·hop·per (gras′hop′ər), an insect with wings and strong hind legs for jumping. *noun.*

grudge (gruj), **1** ill will; angry feeling against; dislike of long standing. **2** to envy the possession of. 1 *noun,* 2 *verb,* **grudg·es, grudged, grudging.**

hatch·ling (hach′ling), a young animal that is born from an egg. *noun.*

Ho·pi (hō′pē), a member of a tribe of American Indians living in northern Arizona. *noun, plural* **Ho·pi** or **Ho·pis.**

ho·ri·zon (hə rī′zn), **1** the line where earth and sky seem to meet. You cannot see beyond the horizon. **2** the limit of one's thinking, experience, interest, or outlook. *noun.*

hor·rid (hôr′id), **1** causing great fear; frightful: *a horrid car accident.* **2** very unpleasant. *adjective.*

il·lu·mi·nate (i lü′mə nāt), **1** to light up; make bright. **2** to make clear; explain. *verb,* **il·lu·mi·nates, il·lu·mi·nat·ed, il·lu·mi·nat·ing.**

med·i·cine (med′ə sən), **1** a substance, such as a drug, used to treat, prevent, or cure disease. **2** the science of treating, preventing, or curing disease and improving health: *Doctors study medicine. noun.*

mesa

me·sa (mā′sə), a high, steep hill that has a flat top and stands alone. A mesa is usually larger and steeper than a butte. *noun.*

mist·y (mis'tē), **1** covered with mist: *misty hills.* **2** not clearly seen; vague; indistinct. *adjective,* **mist·i·er, mist·i·est.**

mourn·ful (môrn'fəl), full of grief; sad; sorrowful. *adjective.*

mourn·ful·ly (môrn'fəl ē), in a mournful manner. *adverb.*

o·cean·og·ra·pher (ō'shə nog'rə fər), a scientist who studies the oceans and seas and the living things in them. *noun.*

of·fer (ô'fər), **1** to hold out to be taken or refused; present: *to offer one's hand.* **2** to be willing if another approves: *They offered to help.* **3** to propose; suggest: *to offer a price. verb.*

or·ches·tra (ôr'kə strə), **1** the musicians playing at a concert, an opera, or a play. **2** the violins, flutes, oboes, and other instruments played together by the musicians in an orchestra. *noun.*

orchestra—the Chicago Symphony Orchestra

per·sist (pər sist'), **1** to refuse to stop or be changed. **2** to last; stay; endure: *On some mountains snow persists all year. verb.*

per·son·al·i·ty (pėr'sə nal'ə tē), **1** the personal or individual quality that makes one person be different or act differently from another: *Her warm, friendly personality attracts many friends.* **2** a well-known person. *noun, plural* **per·son·al·i·ties.**

per·suade (pər swād'), to win over to do or believe; make willing or sure by urging or arguing. *verb,* **per·suades, per·suad·ed, per·suad·ing.**

re·ceiv·er (ri sē'vər), **1** a person who receives: *The receiver of a gift should thank the sender.* **2** a part of the telephone held to the ear. **3** a device that receives sounds, or sounds and pictures, sent by radio waves: *a radio receiver, a television receiver. noun.*

re·cit·al (ri sī'tl), **1** a telling of facts in detail; account. **2** a musical entertainment. *noun.*

re·lief (ri lēf'), **1** the lessening of, or freeing from, a pain, burden, or difficulty: *It was a relief to hear I had passed the test.* **2** something that lessens or frees from pain, burden, or difficulty; aid; help. **3** freedom from a post of duty. *noun.*

re·serve (ri zėrv'), **1** keep back; hold back: *reserve judgment.* **2** set apart. **3** save for use later. **4** anything kept back for future use; store: *reserve supplies for winter.* **1-3,** *verb,* **re·served, re·serv·ing; 4** *noun.*

re·source·ful (ri sôrs′fəl), good at thinking of ways to do things. *adjective.*

a hat	i it	oi oil	ch child	ə stands for:
ā age	ī ice	ou out	ng long	a in about
ä far	o hot	u cup	sh she	e in taken
e let	ō open	ù put	th thin	i in pencil
ē equal	ô order	ü rule	ᴛʜ then	o in lemon
ėr term			zh measure	u in circus

smol·der (smōl′dər), **1** to burn and smoke without flame: *The campfire smoldered for hours after the blaze died down.* **2** to exist or continue without being let out or expressed. *verb.*

sod (sod), **1** any ground covered with grass. **2** a piece or layer of this containing the grass and its roots: *Some pioneer families lived in houses made of sod called soddies.* **3** to cover with sods: *We had the bare spots on our lawn sodded.* 1, 2 *noun,* 3 *verb.*

sod (definition 2) a **sod** house

spir·it (spir′it), **1** the soul. **2** a human being's moral, religious, or emotional nature. **3** a supernatural being. Ghosts and fairies are spirits. **4 spirits, a** state of mind; disposition; temper. **b** strong alcoholic liquor. **5** to carry away or off secretly. 1-4 *noun,* 5 *verb.*

threat·en (thret′n), **1** to make a threat against; say what will be done to hurt or punish. **2** to give warning of coming trouble. *verb.*

trance (trans), **1** a condition somewhat like sleep in which a person no longer responds to the surroundings. **2** a condition like daydreaming or a trance. *noun.*

trans·mit·ter (tran smit′ər), a device that sends out sounds, or sounds and pictures, by radio waves or by electric current. *noun.*

trop·i·cal (trop′ə kəl), of or like the tropics: *tropical heat. adjective.*

trop·ics (trop′iks), regions near the equator. The hottest parts of the earth are in the tropics. *noun, plural.*

tu·tor (tü′tər *or* tyü′tər), **1** a private teacher. **2** to teach; instruct. 1 *noun.* 2 *verb.*

vi·o·lin (vī′ə lin′), a musical instrument with four strings played with a bow. *noun.*

wa·ter·proof (wô′tər prüf′), able to keep water from coming through: *Umbrellas are waterproof. adjective.*

wa·ter·tight (wô′tər tīt′), so tight that no water can get in or out: *We loaded our canoe with watertight containers. adjective.*

Acknowledgments

Text

Page 6: From *The Kid in the Red Jacket* by Barbara Park. Copyright © 1987 by Barbara Park. Reprinted by permission of Alfred A. Knopf, Inc.

Page 20: "Two Friends" from *Spin a Soft Black Song* by Nikki Giovanni. Copyright © 1971, 1985 by Nikki Giovanni. Reprinted by permission of Farrar, Straus and Giroux, Inc.

Page 21: "Winter Poem" from *My House* by Nikki Giovanni. Copyright © 1972 by Nikki Giovanni. Reprinted by permission of William Morrow & Company, Inc./Publishers, New York.

Page 22: "No Talking!" by Nikki Giovanni. Copyright © by Nikki Giovanni, 1991.

Page 24: From *Between Old Friends*. Copyright © 1987 by Katherine Leiner. Reprinted with permission of the publisher, Franklin Watts, Inc.

Page 34: "China's Precious Pandas" by Claire Miller. Copyright © 1989 National Wildlife Federation. Reprinted from the July, 1989, issue of *Ranger Rick Magazine*, with the permission of the publisher, the National Wildlife Federation.

Page 42: "Why We Have Dogs in Hopi Villages" & "How Oceans Came to Be" from *And It Is Still That Way: Legends told by Arizona Indian Children* with notes by Byrd Baylor, 1976, Trails West Press, Santa Fe, NM. Copyright © 1976 Byrd Baylor. Reprinted by permission of the author.

Page 50: "Who's the New Kid with the Hoofs?" from *Humorous Monologues* by Martha Bolton, 1989, pp. 38–42. Copyright © 1989 by Martha Bolton. Reprinted by permission of Sterling Publishing Co., Inc., 387 Park Avenue South, New York, NY 10016.

Page 56: "Early Spring" from *On Bear's Head* by Philip Whalen. Copyright © 1960, 1965, 1969 by Philip Whalen. Reprinted by permission of the author.

Page 57: "Mouse Under the House" from *In for Winter, Out for Spring* by Arnold Adoff. Copyright © 1991 by Arnold Adoff. Reprinted by permission of Harcourt Brace Jovanovich, Inc.

Page 58: *Turtle Watch* by George Ancona. Copyright © 1987 by George Ancona. Reprinted by permission of the author.

Page 76: "About Turtle Watch" by George Ancona. Copyright © by George Ancona, 1991.

Page 80: "The Glittering Cloud" from *On the Banks of Plum Creek* by Laura Ingalls Wilder, pp. 192–204, illustrated by Garth Williams. Text copyright © 1937 by Laura Ingalls Wilder. Copyright © renewed 1963 by Roger L. MacBride. Illustrations copyright © 1953 by Garth Williams, copyright © renewed 1981 by Garth Williams. Reprinted by permission of HarperCollins Publishers.

Page 94: "Trapped" from *Addie Across the Prairie* by Laurie Lawlor. Text copyright © 1986 by Laurie Lawlor. Reprinted by permission of Albert Whitman & Company.

Page 111: "Fraidycat" from *Addie Across the Prairie* by Laurie Lawlor. Text copyright © 1986 by Laurie Lawlor. Reprinted by permission of Albert Whitman & Company.

Artists

Illustrations owned and copyrighted by the illustrator.
Leslie Cober cover, 1–5, 119–123
Lisa Adams 6–17
Gil Ashby 20–23
John Weber (calligraphy) 24–32
Chris Sheban 34, 37 (map), 58, 66
Ruta Daugavietis 43–49
Harry Roolaart 51–55
Garth Williams 80–90
Joel Spector 92–118

Photographs

Unless otherwise acknowledged, all photographs are the property of Scott Foresman.
Page 23: Courtesy Nikki Giovanni
Pages 24 (inset), 27, 29–30, 32: Michael Arthur
Page 35: Spencer Jones/Bruce Coleman, Inc. (inset)
Pages 35, 37, 39–41: George B. Schaller
Page 56: Andersen Windows
Page 59: Adrienne T. Gibson/ANIMALS ANIMALS
Pages 60–63, 64 (inset), 65 (inset), 67–73, 74 (inset), 75 (inset top, inset bottom), 79: George Ancona
Pages 64–65: Backgrounds/West Light
Pages 74–75: Jeff Gnass/West Stock
Page 76: Addison Doty/George Ancona (inset)
Page 78: Pierre Kopp/West Light
Page 91: Don and Pat Valenti
Page 125: Doris DeWitt/Stock Boston (bottom)
Page 126: Courtesy WTTW, Chicago
Page 127: Solomon D. Butcher Collection, Nebraska State Historical Society

Glossary

The contents of the glossary have been adapted from *Beginning Dictionary*, Copyright © 1988 Scott, Foresman and Company and *Intermediate Dictionary*, Copyright © 1988 Scott, Foresman and Company.